THE VALUATION
OF
PROPERTY INVESTMENTS

By the same authors:

Property Valuation Techniques
David Isaac and Terry Steley

Property Finance
David Isaac

Property Development: Appraisal and Finance
David Isaac

Property Investment
David Isaac

Property Companies: Share Price and Net Asset Value
David Isaac and Neil Woodroffe

Urban Economics: A Global Perspective
Paul Balchin, David Isaac and Jean Chen

THE VALUATION OF PROPERTY INVESTMENTS

Sixth Edition
by

NIGEL ENEVER
BSc, FRICS,
Chartered Surveyor
Enever & Co

and

DAVID ISAAC
BSc, MSc, PhD, FRICS
Professor of Real Estate Management
Head of Real Estate and Housing
University of Greenwich

A division of Reed Business Information
ESTATES GAZETTE
151 WARDOUR STREET, LONDON W1F 8BN

First Edition 1977
Second Edition 1981
Third Edition 1984
Fourth Edition 1989
Reprinted 1992
Fifth Edition 1995
Sixth Edition 2002

ISBN 0 7282 03693

In this book, the words 'he' and 'his' should
be understood to include the female gender.

Typeset by Amy Boyle, Rochester
Printed and bound by WS Bookwell, Juva

CONTENTS

To Juliet, Charlotte, Matthew,
Michael and Barbara

Preface to the Sixth Edition

In this edition, the book has been updated and revised to reflect changes in the market, the development of appraisal methods and the subsequent changes in professional practice. The initial overview in Part 1 of the book, The Economic and Legal Framework, has been revised to show the present position. Changes in appraisal techniques have been incorporated in Part II on Investment Valuation. Revisions have also been made in Part III, which examines Investment Appraisal, and a new chapter on Investment Risk has been included.

The book continues to serve a number of purposes, as it has done in the previous five editions. Firstly, it provides a critical examination of valuation techniques with particular reference to the investment method of valuation. Secondly, it supplies practising valuers and appraisers with more effective data, information and techniques to enable them to carry out their valuations, appraisals and negotiations in an increasingly competitive field. Finally, it provides assistance to students in understanding the context of and a range of approaches to the valuation and appraisal of property investments.

Nigel Enever, Brighton
David Isaac, University of Greenwich

September 2001

PART I

THE ECONOMIC AND LEGAL FRAMEWORK

Chapter One

Investment

Investment is the giving up of a capital sum now in exchange for benefits to be received in the future. These will usually take the form of an income flow and/or capital gain. This book is mostly concerned with financial investment by the transfer of existing capital assets. This form of investment is to be distinguished from asset formation by property development.

Since property is only one avenue of investment, and all investment opportunities are in competition for the total of investment funds available, it is necessary throughout this book to consider the comparison of property investments, not only one with another, but with other forms of investment. For the moment it may be noted that there are broadly two forms of financial investment, viz (1) that where money is lent and a debt is created such as the granting of a mortgage or the acquisition of public authority stock, and (2) that where a proprietary interest is acquired such as the acquisition of an interest in property or in a company by becoming a shareholder.

Investment Markets

Different types of investment have different characteristics and may appeal to different types of investor. In practice, only a very small number of investors may be in the market for a particular investment. In this sense, therefore, there is not one investment market but many.

Types of investment include: stocks and shares, which are bought and sold on the Stock Exchange; loans to companies (debentures) and local authorities; insurance policies; unit trusts; property; works of art; durable articles bought for use; and many others. The term 'property' as used in the book generally relates to freehold and leasehold interests in land and buildings, or landed property as it is sometimes known.

The property sector can be broken down into subsectors, in which different classes of purchaser will be interested. It can be subdivided according to type and size, such as small houses at one extreme, and multi-million pound office investments at the other. It can be subdivided according to location: a small industrialist may limit his demand for factory space to a particular area, for example, whereas a pension fund acquiring industrial property for its investment portfolio may be relatively indifferent to the part of the country or region in which the property is located. A particular property may, according to its type, attract demand at a local, a national or even an international level.

Methods of Investing in Property

Acquisition of property is normally termed 'direct' investment as against various means of 'indirect' investment considered below. Property may be acquired by auction, by tender, by private treaty, or by takeover bid. Further variations of 'direct' investment are property development, and 'sale and lease-back'.

To acquire property through property development the investing agency may undertake the development itself, but unless it specialises in this field, it is more likely to come to an arrangement with a specialist. This could be through the investor providing the finance for the development on terms mutually beneficial to both investing institution and developer. The terms will necessarily be such as to compensate for the relatively high risks involved in development. In view of the complexity of the arrangements, property development financing schemes are beyond the scope of this book.

The sale and leaseback transaction arises because an owner-occupier wishes to raise capital. He may therefore dispose of his property to an investing institution who will immediately lease the property back to him. He then continues in occupation as tenant rather than as owner, and is able to invest the capital in his business. This type of transaction may be attractive to industrialists as a cheap way of raising capital in times of high interest rates. It does, of course, have the disadvantages, from their point of view of exchanging a freehold interest for a leasehold interest and of the rent rising periodically to a market value, thereby extinguishing most of the value in the interest.

An alternative means for an owner-occupier or potential owner-occupier to raise capital is to mortgage the property. This would create an indirect property investment for the mortgagee by way of a loan secured on the property. Two further indirect methods of investing in property but where an equity type investment is created are through property bonds, and through shares in property companies.

A property bond is a life assurance scheme similar to unit trust life assurance, but with the premiums and dividends linked to property instead of stocks and shares. As regards shares in property companies, these may be acquired by direct purchase of shares in individual companies on the Stock Exchange or by purchase of unit trusts that hold property shares, generally along with non-property shares in a broad portfolio.

Influences on the Investment Markets

There are numerous influences on the investment markets, the major ones being the development of specialist institutions to convert prospective purchasers into actual purchasers, and the many means by which the government exerts its influence. The special institutions referred to include the building societies which enable individuals to convert income into capital for house-purchase. The Agricultural Mortgage Corporation performs a similar function in the agricultural land market.

Although it may be said that the markets for occupation and investment are separate, this is not entirely true. The easier such special institutions make it for occupiers to acquire property, the less willing they will be to rent it, and thus the lower will be the supply of rented accommodation for investment. In the commercial and industrial fields, more and more banks and financial institutions are willing to lend to enable industrialists to acquire freeholds rather than having to rent. In the 'pure' investment field, the property bonds have been developed, which allow individuals who could not independently afford to invest in commercial property to combine together with others for that purpose.

Concerning the second major influence on the markets generally, the government can influence interest rates and thereby the activities of investors, through open market operations, by having an effect on the base rates and through its borrowing requirements. In the 1970s the government also intervened very positively in the form of counter-inflation measures. In the context of a mixed economy, it may also affect investment decisions by less direct means, such as general or selective policies relating to grants, loans, taxation, planning and security of tenure.

Returns on Investment

The income generated or the capital gain achieved from an investment can be measured by converting it to a percentage of the capital outlay. This percentage is normally calculated on an annual basis and is referred to as the rate of interest or discount rate. A capital gain can be described in terms of an annual discount rate by calculating the rate of compound interest required to achieve a certain capital gain over a given period of time.

In the case of property investment, if the property is purchased for letting, the returns will be in the form of rental income and/or capital appreciation. If it is purchased for occupation, the return will be in the form of savings in rental outgoing. Again, capital appreciation may feature.

The initial yield on an investment is the current net income expressed as a percentage of the capital value. This initial yield is sometimes known as the *flat yield*, *straight yield*, or *running yield*. The current income is normally known or can be estimated, and therefore capital value of the investment depends upon the yield which investors are prepared to accept.

Investors seek the highest rate of return on their capital. This is not to say that they seek the highest initial yield. They may accept a low yield because of the long-term prospects of the investment. To some extent the yield reflects the investors' views about the future risks attached to the investment. The higher the yield, the higher the risks and problems associated with an investment, and vice versa. Thus, another term for this initial yield is the all risks yield, meaning it tries to take these risks into account.

The rate of return on a particular investment is determined by the forces of supply and demand within the market, and is evaluated by investors and their advisers by comparing returns from various investments. There are, however, certain underlying economic influences on the rate of return, and these are considered briefly below.

Even in times of zero inflation, an investor will require a return, however small, for foregoing consumption. In times of inflation, however, he will hope also to be compensated for any erosion of his capital and income. The rate of return required from the investment will also be affected by the incidence of taxation as it differentiates between types of investment, classes of investor, and between the types of return, eg income or capital gain.

In addition to these all-pervading influences – inflation and taxation – there are more specific risks and problems which affect the rates of return on various investments. The risks may be categorised as follows:

(i) The possibility of actual loss of capital as, for example, through bankruptcy or a crash on the investment market.

(ii) The possibility of loss of income. This is very closely associated with (i).

(iii) The risk of irregularity of income, eg because a company is unable to declare a dividend regularly through unprofitability.

Other influences on the rate of return, which are not strictly speaking risks, but are more in the nature of problems which have to be overcome by work, time or expenditure in relation to the investment concerned include the following:

(i) The liquidity of the investment, ie the ease with which it can be converted into cash.

(ii) The costs of transfer (sale and purchase).

(iii) The cost and trouble of management.

Fixed-Interest Securities

Having considered in broad outline how various factors affect the returns on investments, it is now appropriate to consider which factors are particularly relevant to various types of investment and how these factors combine together to determine yields in each case.

Securities is the Stock Exchange term for stocks and shares in general. The largest single issuer of securities is the Government. *Gilts* represent money borrowed by the Government on which it pays a fixed rate of interest – that is the amount payable each year during the life of the stock is always the same, whatever happens to market interest rates during that time. Similar securities are issued by Local Authorities, Public Boards and by Companies, such as stocks, bonds, loans and debentures.

Gilts or gilt-edged securities are issued at a *nominal* or *face* value of £100. When selling at a price of £100 they are selling at *par* (or face) value; over £100 they are selling above par; at less than £100 they are selling below par. Each stock, when issued, will bear a specific fixed interest rate expressed as a percentage of nominal value. This is the stock's *coupon* rate.

Any purchaser of stock can expect to receive the very next interest payment until the stock goes *ex-dividend*. This means that the interest (dividend) payment is imminent and will be paid to those registered stock holders on a specified date. The new purchaser therefore cannot receive a dividend payment until the subsequent date. Interest on most stocks is paid every six months. Prices can be calculated either on this basis or on a *cum* dividend basis (ie including forthcoming dividend).

Gilt-edged securities are basically of two types; those where the government promises to pay back the original capital at a certain date or within a certain range of dates, and which are known as *dated* or *redeemable* stocks; and those where the government makes no promise to pay them back and which are known as *undated* or *irredeemable* stocks. Dated stocks may be categorised according to the length of time to redemption viz:

(i)   shorts – redeemable within five years;
(ii) mediums – with between five and 10 years to redemption; and
(iii) longs – these stocks have a fixed life exceeding 10 years.

When a new stock is issued the government has to offer the current market rate of interest in order to attract investors. In the immediate post-war period this was as low as 2.5% for undated stock, but in times of higher inflation this rate of interest on government stock has been more in the region of 10%. Those investors who bought the 2.5% undated stock (Consolidated stocks or Consols as they are known) continue to receive £2.50 per annum for each £100 invested. They can dispose of their investment on the Stock Exchange. A potential investor today might then be faced with the choice of new investments yielding say 10% or the 2.5% stock. The market price of the latter would then be determined by the yield which can be obtained on the former. The new investor would be fairly indifferent as to whether he bought new stock or old provided that the yield was the same. In order for the stock to yield 10%, its price would have to be reduced from the original £100 as follows:

$$£2.50 \times \frac{100}{10} = £25$$

Check on yield: $\frac{2.50}{25} \times 100 = 10\%$

Hence if interest rates rise, the value of stock diminishes, and conversely if interest rates fall the value increases. It would only pay the government to redeem the stock in this example if interest rates fell below 2.5%, because it would otherwise then be paying a rate of interest higher than it would need to pay on a new issue.

The calculation of yield on dated stock is more complicated. If the government promised to repay the original £100 in the above example three years hence, the market value of the stock would clearly be in excess of £25. In addition to the £2.50 per annum income, the potential purchaser would have to take into account the capital gain he would make on redemption. The resultant yield is known as the *gross redemption yield,* and the means of calculating it are considered further in Chapter 13.

It has already been stated that a new investor would be fairly indifferent towards choosing between a newly issued stock and the 2.5% Consol provided that the relative prices were such as to make the yield the same. There are in fact slight differences in yield between types of stock. For example, shorts tend to command a lower rate of interest than longer dated stocks due to the lower risks of variation in their value.

The rate of interest on undated gilt-edged securities is reckoned to be a good starting point for comparing rates of interest on other forms of investment. It is one of the few types of investment where the future income in nominal terms is known with absolute certainty.

Shares

There are two main types of share, each of which represent part ownership of a company and the right to participate in its profits in the form of dividends. These two types are preference shares and ordinary shares. The former provide a fixed return on capital paid out of profits. Ordinary shares also earn a share in profits for their owner, but in this case the dividend is variable as it represents the 'risk' capital after the other investors and creditors have been paid. This type of share is known as an 'equity', and the term 'equity' is sometimes used to describe any 'risk' type investment including property investments. In a good year an ordinary shareholder should receive a relatively high dividend, and in a very poor year he may receive no dividend at all. As profits vary, there is therefore no stability of income, and yield is calculated on the current dividend.

Yields vary enormously, and in deciding which companies to invest in and the yield which would be acceptable, investors must have regard to a number of factors. They must try to forecast future profitability, and this will entail a study of the particular industry and company concerned. They must then consider the company's policies with regard to distribution of profits and *gearing*. The 'gearing' of a company relates to the proportion of profits taken up by interest payments. Basically, the more profits a company ploughs back into the business, ie the less it distributes and the lower its gearing, the more secure is the future income, and the lower the yield.

Technically, gearing is the relationship between loan capital (debentures, mortgages, preference shares) and equity capital (ordinary share stock), which in practice is usually expressed as a ratio or percentage of loan capital to total capital. In forecasting the future gearing of a company, regard will be had to the likelihood or otherwise of any rights being exercised to convert loan stock etc into ordinary shares. Leverage is the American term used for gearing.

Gearing can operate in both directions, ie in a rising market the equity-holder's share rises faster than the market, but in a falling market, such as existed in the early 1990s, the reverse happens and the equity-holder suffers. At such time the position of the equity-holder may be safeguarded to varying degrees, according to circumstances, by degearing where practicable, eg either by buying in the loan capital in the market or by a scheme of arrangements with the holder of the loan capital.

The *price to earnings ratio* (P/E) is the market value of the *equity shares* in a company divided by the annual earnings of that company. The *earnings yield* is the inverse of this ratio. This should be differentiated from the *dividend yield*. This former relates the earnings of the company (which can be derived from an analysis of the company's latest annual report) to the value of the shares. The dividend yield on the other hand relates the income paid to shareholders in the form of dividends to the value of the shares. The dividend yield will usually be lower than the earnings yield because a company may be retaining sums in reserve for payment of debts or future expansion. The relationship between these two types of yield may be calculated. Thus if a company whose equity yield is 12% pays an 8% dividend, the dividend is 1.5 times covered by the earnings. This is referred to as the *dividend cover*. An investor may regard a low dividend yield as acceptable if there is a high earnings yield. This may be because the company is investing money which will provide future growth for these shares. Net asset value is also a relevant factor in valuing shares, particularly property investment company shares.

The Reverse Yield Gap

In the days of relatively low inflation and interest rates – broadly speaking before 1960 – equity-type investments, generally representing a greater risk than fixed interest securities, produced higher yields. Some shares, such as some mining shares, are still regarded as high risk and produce correspondingly high yields. After the early 1960s, however, the risk which came to dominate all others and to have therefore the greatest effect on the yield was the erosion of income and capital by inflation. Hence investments where the income could not adjust to inflation such as gilt-edged securities, tended to provide higher yields than those which could adjust. This phenomenon became known as the 'reserve yield gap', and during the 1970s varied between about 3% and 8%.

In the late 1980s inflation was back down to about 7% in accordance with the Retail Price Index (RPI). High interest rates have formed part of the Government's policy in maintaining low inflation by attempting to curb borrowing. Accordingly, the bank base rate was around 14%. The Financial Times Stock Index showed the ordinary *dividend yield* to be 4.77%. Prime shop investments were yielding 5%. These low yields in equity type investments represent the anticipation of real growth to compensate for the loss of short-term earnings which could otherwise have been obtained by investing in Government Stocks at say 90% or other similarly high yielding fixed interest investments. It is this loss of short-term earnings or initial yield which, when taken over the investment market as a whole, is represented by the reverse yield gap. In fact such an investor will require a rate of return including growth not only sufficient to compensate for loss of initial yield, but also sufficient to compensate for other risks of equities as against fixed interest securities.

The type of property which most big investors consider suitable for their portfolio is commercial property let subject to frequent reviews, say every five years. Income from property, therefore, like equity dividend is reviewable (and thereby hedged against inflation), although less frequently than in the latter case. One further point is that rent ranks above debenture interest and equity dividend for payment on liquidation. These three types of investment are ranked in this order with the most secure at the bottom of the diagram at Figure 1.1, and the shaded areas show the extent to which the income may grow or remain fixed.

In this illustration, if the equities and debentures are held in the same company which occupies the property comprised in the property investment, then in the event of the company going into liquidation and in the worst situation despite rent being a prior charge, it may not be possible to retrieve arrears of rent. But the property will still be there even if the company is not, and the property investment capital, if the property can be relet, is therefore in this sense the most secure of any of the investments.

In the case of equities, there is no knowing in advance precisely when the dividend will be varied, and the possibility of the dividend varying so frequently means that, at least in theory (and depending on the particular shares in practice), there is little or no stability of income. Property investments, on the other hand, usually provide for rent reviews at regular intervals, say every five years. Thus the timing of future variations of income is known precisely, there is usually stability of income between reviews, and

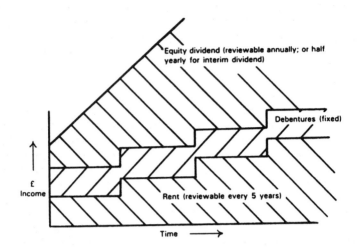

Figure 1.1

the length of time between reviews is such that in many cases the income will not be affected by short-term economic fluctuations.

Other Non-Property Investments

Other investments already referred to include insurance policies, unit trusts, and durable articles bought for use. These all have different characteristics and are all suitable for the small investor.

Other forms of investment include, for example, commodities, precious metals and works of art. Although they provide no income, works of fine art and rare stamps have provided spectacular capital appreciation for their owners, and have become accepted in some quarters as suitable vehicles for institutional investment.

Owner-Occupier and Investment Markets

The owner-occupier sector has tended to be overlooked in property texts, except those of a macro-economic nature. The problem lies with the fact that there is a substantial investment market in the UK where properties are developed for lease and sale and it is this activity that is the most traditional approach for property developers in the property markets. This is unlike the situation in the European markets where development is more likely to be for the purpose of owner-occupation.

Owner-occupation is also much more important in emerging economies and in economies in transition from non-market forms. Analysis of the development of property investment markets in Eastern Europe, for instance, provides a clear indication that owner-occupiers give a kick-start to the development and investment markets, especially where they are overseas companies or individual investors. In Hungary, the Czech Republic and Poland there is evidence that as economies have opened up from state control so overseas operators have wanted to establish plants. The investment market initially was non-existent, as was local finance for any projects. These are two of the necessary precursors for the development of property markets and, interestingly, often the two elements missing in emerging economies or economies in transition from a command to a market economy. China is another example of this problem. What happens in these situations is that the foreign company usually sets up a partnership arrangement with local producers, for instance a joint venture. Then, the problem arises that there are no suitable premises available, so they build them (in these cases they act as developer and kick-start the development market). In addition, as local finance is not forthcoming, they need to obtain this from their home market or international sources. This leads to an injection of overseas capital, thus starting up the local financial market. As the company expands and requires more or different premises so they buy and sell buildings, thus starting the investment market especially where they have to retain old premises for re-letting as there are few owner-occupiers with capital to purchase. Success of such operations can then encourage rather real estate activity, for instance profit from land sales may, in a rapidly improving market, prove to be a more important contribution to profit than sales of the product, especially if the economy is emerging slowly. The role of the overseas company thus could be influential in the development, investment and financial sectors. Also, overseas agents might arrive to ensure the system starts to work properly. Evidence from Eastern European countries mentioned previously suggests that while Germany, French and Italian companies may be taking the lead in investment and finance, UK firms dominate the agency business.[1]

A final point that applies both to emerging and established economies, is the nature of finance. In a period of boom and slump in property markets, finance can have a major effect. If money is easy to come by at cheaper rates, this can have an effect on development and investment activity and can lead to inflation of prices and a boom situation. The property boom of the late 1980s was fuelled by bank finance mainly from overseas and foreign banks. The bubble in the Japanese economy in the late 1980s was also fuelled by easy bank finance. A scheme referred to by some as 'property pin-ball' suggested that banks generated the inflation in values by constantly arranging for the buying and selling of the same property with appropriate increases in value. The banks benefited from the fees on the transactions but also provided the inflated valuations so that the process could carry on until the bubble burst, leading to the collapse of the property market and three major banks becoming insolvent.

The property market is sometimes held to be inefficient; if it is inefficient then prices and values will differ. Research in the UK has suggested that overall the market may not be inefficient and that market knowledge is reflected in the prices, so values will be close to prices.[2] Traditionally though, in most sectors of the market, the view has been taken that the market is inefficient. There are a number of reasons for inefficiency:

- lack of data on market transactions
- lack of homogeneity in property assets – they are all different and thus difficult to value
- lack of liquidity in the market.

This is covered in more detail in Chapter 2.

Lack of Liquidity in the Property Market

This is specifically due to a number of conditions in the market, namely:

- high transaction and entry costs to the market, lotting problems (property is sold in expensive lot sizes), the size of lots and their indivisibility
- lack of transactions, meaning that valuation is difficult
- lack of a market infrastructure, so transactions are slow to complete
- lack of a central market place, so there are only localised markets
- legal problems in the nature of registering land and ensuring the registers contain any debts against the asset and the proof of title.

References

1 Balchin, P.N., Isaac, D. and Chen, J. *Urban Economics: A Global Perspective*, Palgrave, 2000.
2 Brown, G.R. *Property Investment and the Capital Markets*, E & FN Spon, 1991.

Further Reading

An Introduction to Buying and Selling Shares, Information and Press Dept, The Stock Exchange.
'Mainly for Students: Investment Terms', 273EG 311.
'Mainly for Students: Stock Exchange Glossary of Terms', 281EG 319.

Chapter Two

The Property Market

Having established that property is in competition with other forms of investment, we shall now move on to consider the special characteristics of property, if any, which distinguish it from these other investments. The concept of perfect competition is familiar to students of economics. In economic theory, the perfectly competitive market requires that the following conditions (amongst others) should exist:

(i) Buyers and sellers must have precise knowledge of prices being paid elsewhere;

(ii) The product in the market must be homogeneous;

(iii) There must be perfect mobility in the market, with buyers and sellers willing and able to move to make a purchase and the new product must be mobile as well; and

(iv) There must be so many buyers and sellers in the market that no one individual on his own can influence market price.

Competition in the land market is far from perfect. Such imperfections include, for example, the immobility of the product and the possibility of low numbers of buyers and sellers – in extreme circumstances there may be only one potential purchaser, commonly referred to as a 'special purchaser'. Certain distinctive features of a property interest may create a situation in which the seller has almost monopolistic powers. Even if relatively identical units of property exist, they will not necessarily be offered for sale simultaneously. Discussed below are the other main distinguishing features of property as an investment.

Distinguishing Features of Property

Heterogeneity

It is easy to fall into the trap of discussing investment in property as one would that of investing in a building society or on the Stock Exchange. To do so is to overlook the fact that property is infinitely more heterogeneous than other investment media. Every property occupies a unique location, for example, and there are many other instances of possible differences, including design, condition, size, aspect and so on. It is true that some properties, such as semi-detached suburban houses, are close substitutes for one another, but on the other hand it is also true that a certain type of property, such as a Scottish island, may present very rare opportunities for acquisition and therefore be virtually unique as an investment opportunity. As an aside, it can be noted that in certain circumstances an over-dependence on location as a valuable attribute may make a particular class of property abnormally vulnerable to adjacent changes and development such as road works, traffic management and shopping schemes.

Indivisibility

Another feature of property which distinguishes it from most other investments is its frequent indivisibility and the relatively high cost of each indivisible unit. This often results in property being unattainable as an investment medium for the small investor, except for his own occupation, or through acquiring shares in property companies, property bonds or other indirect means. It also results in the frequent use of credit in purchasing property, which may be supplied by building societies, banks or possibly insurance companies and pension funds. Thus changes in the availability of credit may have profound effects on the property market.

Inelasticity of Supply

A fundamental economic feature of property is the difficulty of varying its supply. The physical overall supply of land is virtually fixed, and the mix of various land uses is difficult to alter, because of planning controls. Due to the time taken to obtain planning permission, arrange finance, construct buildings and arrange disposals, the development industry is slow to respond to an increase in demand. Conversely it is difficult for supply to react to a reduction in demand. It is not always viable or practicable to demolish or change buildings to meet such a reduction. This lack of responsiveness (or inelasticity of supply) in the industry leaves it abnormally vulnerable to economic booms and slumps. When the market is already booming it is too late for a developer to respond. By the time he has done so, the boom will be over. An over-supply at this stage will actually worsen a slump.

High Costs of Transfer

The incidental costs of dealing in property are high relative to those of other investments. Investigation of title, the need for a formal contract and the frequent need to create a mortgage are reasons for employing a solicitor, while the desirability of a professional opinion of value, of a report upon physical condition, or to appoint an agent to handle advertising and negotiations, all add to the cost of transfer. There are also taxes on transfer such as stamp duty.

Special Problems of Management

Due to the complicated economic and legal problems associated with property investment, particular regard to management is required. This may take time, experience, expertise and/or money on the part of the investor. Where repairing liabilities fall upon the landlord, these problems are compounded. This is very different to the investment in gilt-edged stock where a cheque falls through the letter box or a direct credit transfer is made every six months.

Special Risks

These include:

(i)   Physical risks such as fire, earthquake, flooding, wear and tear and user damage.
(ii) The risk of liability to third parties due to defective premises.
(iii) The financial risk of granting leases for specified periods of time with or without reviews.
(iv) The economic risk that a property will become obsolete in terms of design or purpose.

It should be noted that with the exception of deterioration due to wear and tear, the first two risks mentioned above can be insured against. However, there is still a slight residual risk of under insurance or omission to insure.

Perpetuity

At the risk of stating the axiomatic, it may be said that land is durable and it is the human habitat and the space in which economic wealth is generated and so the person who owns part of it has an investment in something which always has been and always will be absolutely essential to economic needs.

These economic needs relate to the fact that property is a factor of production and thus is the space in which the production process takes place. Economic theory tells us that land is combined with other factors – labour, capital and enterprise – to produce economic wealth and thus land is at the core of this activity.

The issue of durability is something that requires clarification. It should be noted here that the value of property includes both the land and the buildings and these elements are not separated in the calculation done. As will be explained later, essentially it would only be a cost approach to valuation that might attempt such separation. Thus, it is land that is durable and scarce, not the building on it (except in examples of prestigious design or historic importance). The building is susceptible to depreciation (wearing out and requiring replacement) and obsolescence (arising from changes in the economic and social environment which make the current use of the building redundant). In these circumstances, it can be seen that it is the land element which is likely to grow and appreciate in value in the long term. Most analysis that valuers undertake does not distinguish between these two elements.

Imperfect Knowledge

Transactions involving certain types of property are infrequent and the details concerning them are kept secret. This leads to lack of information (for the general public, if not for the handful of professionals closely concerned) about transactions in certain sectors of the market. To counter this point, however, there is now an increasing stream of generalised information about transactions and the state of the market appearing in the professional press. Much debate has arisen on the relative efficiency of the market.

Decentralised Market

The stock market uses computer screens to centralise prices in the same way that it previously used a centralised dealing floor, but this central market is not evident for property. Property is normally bought and sold through agents acting in, and familiar with, a particular locality. The exception to this is with regard to the major firms, mainly in London, who operate nationally and even internationally in the purchase and sale of investments for major clients, particularly the institutions. However, these firms also have staff familiar with regional locations.

Government Intervention

In view of the political significance of property, government intervention is rife. The following list gives an indication of some of the main forms that this may take:

(a) rent control and security of tenure, now more historic;
(b) discriminatory taxation and reliefs from taxation;
(c) control of credit;
(d) control of land use and control of the construction, maintenance and use of buildings;
(e) compulsory purchase and public development; and
(f) attempts to solve the compensation/betterment problem.

Many of these points are legal, and this taken together with the variety of interests which can exist in property, means that special knowledge of the law is necessary either by the investor or by his professional advisors.

In considering legislation further, it is apparent that this falls into two categories: firstly, that which has a general application, and, secondly, that which affects individual classes of property and investor differently. Examples of the first type of legislation are: The Town and Country Planning Acts; the Building Regulations; the law of compulsory purchase; and the Defective Premises Act.

As regards specific legislation relating to residential and agricultural property, this is dealt with in the sections on these sectors of the market further on in this chapter. The most relevant of such specific legislation, however, in the context of this book, relates to the commercial sector, and it is thought appropriate to deal with this briefly at this stage.

In the commercial sector, tenants are given *security of tenure*; under the Landlord and Tenant Act 1954, Part II, they may apply for a new lease at the expiration of the existing one, at a rent which ignores the effect of any qualifying improvements they have carried out or goodwill they have established. If, on the other hand, the landlord has grounds for obtaining possession, the tenant may be entitled to compensation for disturbance under this Act and/or for improvements under the Landlord and Tenant Act 1927, Part I. Apart from ignoring the effect of tenants' improvements and goodwill in assessing a new rent, there is no general control of rents in the commercial sector. There was an exception to this for a short while when a 'freeze' was imposed as a counter-inflation measure from 1972 to 1975.

Before leaving the subject of legislation, there is one further area to consider. This concerns legislation which operates selectively towards different classes of investor. The primary example is *taxation*. Different classes of investor may be subject to different rates of tax according to their circumstances, and certain classes, such as insurance companies, pension funds and charities may be treated favourably or be exempt.

The Ability to Create Interests in Property

An interest in property may be defined as a 'bundle of rights' over that property, and it is these interests in property which are bought and sold rather than the actual properties themselves.

The highest form of ownership, which is the largest bundle of rights and is of permanent duration, is the *freehold interest*. The expression 'freehold' is colloquially used synonymously with the legal term 'fee simple'. In fact the 'fee simple' is only one variety of freehold interest.

A freeholder is said to hold the property 'absolutely and in perpetuity'. He may be 'in possession' of the property or he may have foregone the right to possession (occupation) by letting it as an investment. In the latter case, he will be entitled to possession on the expiration of the tenancy, and this is described as the landlord's *reversion*. As has been seen, the ability to gain the reversion may be affected by legislation.

Normally, freehold interests are acquired by the payment of a single capital sum. Occasionally, however, the vendor may take part of the consideration in the form of a perpetual annual income known as a rentcharge.

Although the freehold interest is the most powerful of the interests, it is nevertheless subject to restrictions, some of which are comparatively recent in origin. Some of these have been referred to already and include: regulations, for example, relating to building and land use; liability to compulsory purchase; easements, such as rights of way; restrictive covenants, which may, for example, prohibit development; and the law of nuisance.

A *leasehold interest* is created out of a freehold interest, and is therefore of necessity less powerful than the latter. It is of limited duration and is subject to covenants, which may be of a positive or negative nature. The consideration consists, in part or in full, of a periodic payment. If this represents the full annual value relating to the land and the building, it is termed the *rack rent*, and if relating to the site only, it is termed the *ground rent*. If it does not represent the full annual value, it may be because a single capital payment (*premium*) is made in addition, or because the tenant has undertaken improvements or immediate repairs, or because the lease was granted some years earlier and the rent is out of date.

The leaseholder may in turn create a lesser interest by underletting the premises, in which event he becomes known as the *head lessee* paying a *head rent*. This process may continue 'down the line', and a whole 'chain' of interests may be built up.

The lease terms and the quality of the tenant are important in assessing the merits of an investment, and in the case of leasehold investments, due to the wasting nature of leases, consideration may need to be given to the provision of a sinking fund.

In addition to the division in a vertical plane, interests in the same property may be created 'side by side' or horizontally, as for example by the freehold interest being shared by two or more persons, who are then said to have *joint tenancies* or *tenancies-in-common*.

Finally, and somewhat unusually, it is possible to create an interest for the life of a person, or persons, or for it to commence after the life of one or more persons, possibly contingent upon some other event. Such interests are known as *life interests*.

Sectors of the Property Market

Ground Rents

A ground rent is a rent payable under a ground lease. This may be created under a development scheme whereby the developer is granted a ground lease. Until the buildings are erected, the investment is termed an *unsecured ground rent*; thereafter it is termed *secured*. There may be an intermediate lessee holding a leasehold ground rent investment.

This type of investment lagged behind others in the introduction of the practice of incorporating rent reviews into the lease. For this reason, and because they are long leases, there are many such investments without reviews or with very infrequent reviews. Such investments are similar to fixed-interest securities. The income is secured on a property the annual value of which may exceed the ground rent by many times. In this sense there is a similar degree of certainty of payment as in the case of gilt-edged stocks. They have the disadvantage over gilts of being less liquid (they cannot be bought and sold on the Stock Exchange) and of being more troublesome to manage, but they have they potential advantages of a reversion and the possibilities of merging the interest with that of the lessee or renegotiating the terms of the lease. With property there is always the possibility of making a gain on redevelopment once possession is obtained. Another factor to be considered is that although the lessee is unlikely to default, he may be constantly in arrears with the rent. This would not apply with the income from gilts.

The overall effect of these factors is for such ground rents to command a similar yield to gilts although usually somewhat higher to reflect additional risk, unless there is an immediate or foreseeable prospect of making a capital gain by one of the means considered above.

In the residential sector it is often desirable or necessary, as in the case of flats, for a developer to dispose of the units by way of long lease rather than freehold. In order to make these as attractive as possible to potential purchasers the ground rent is usually set very low and reviewed infrequently, if at all, and then usually by a fairly nominal predetermined amount. The investments thereby created may command yields considerably above gilts in view of the relatively high costs of dealing with small property investments, and the protection afforded in certain instances to lessees under the Landlord and Tenant Act 1954, Part I and the Leasehold Reform Act 1967. Under the latter piece of legislation, qualifying lessees with long leasehold interests in houses are given the opportunity of compulsorily acquiring the freehold interest or obtaining an extended lease, sometimes on advantageous terms. Lessees of flats may also now be able to claim the right to buy (Housing Act 1988). The Leasehold Reform, Housing and Urban Development Act 1993 gives lessees of blocks of flats collectively the right to acquire the freehold of the block providing certain criteria are met. These criteria include the proviso that at least two-thirds of the qualifying lessees in the block should be in favour of collective enfranchisement. In appropriate cases, the lessees can grant themselves a 999-year lease at a peppercorn rent.

The usual pattern for new ground leases in the commercial sector is for the rent to be 'geared' to the rack rent of the premises erected on the site. Such gearing normally entails the ground rent being reviewed at the same time as the rack rent and rising proportionally by the same amount. Such investments bear similar qualities to rack rents in terms of growth, but are more secure. They are therefore likely to show yields slightly below the rack rents to which they are geared.

Shops

Shops vary substantially in size and type, from the out-of-town hypermarket, through the good class High Street shop, to the dwindling number of grocery and provision stores round the corner.

The most important factor governing the investment potential of a shop is its position. However, it is virtually impossible to make general comments about what is and what is not a good position, because factors will vary from town to town. The one exception to this probably relates to the position of the shop in a group of shops. Adjoining 'dead' frontages such as banks and offices is disadvantageous, whereas proximity to a large store 'magnet' is usually an advantage. If the goods sold in the shop are consumer durables then it is likely that customers prefer to compare the goods with those in other shops, and therefore it is usually desirable if such shops are grouped together.

Because the position is so important, it follows that a large proportion of the value of a prime shop is in its site. The prime shopping frontages in London are traditionally in the area of Oxford Street between Oxford Circus and Bond Street station. This is a comparatively small area with a huge market of potential shoppers, and the rents and values achieved reflect the fact. A rent for a standard shop unit on this frontage could be up to fifty or more times the rent on a similar size unit in other parts of London.

As a result of these factors, the supply of High Street shops is very inelastic. The principal demand is for *Zone 'A'* space. This is the front part of the shop (generally a 6-metre depth). The demand cannot be satisfied by either vertical development or by extending the shop depth.

This fact that a large element of the value is in the site has its advantages and its disadvantages for the investor. It has the advantage, as with ground rent investments, that land is virtually indestructible and an investment therein is accordingly secure. On the other hand, it has the disadvantage of vulnerability to changes affecting the value of the position. For example, the imposition of new parking restrictions in the area or the development of a competing shopping centre or hypermarket could affect the desirability of a once prime position, and accordingly the effect on value would be proportionately greater than in the case of a property which did not depend so much on position. In practice, however, a prime pitch in a particular location may be regarded as stable due to long-established and relatively unchanging patterns of pedestrian flow.*

Another important factor is the tenant's covenant, ie the quality of the tenant or the ability of the tenant to fulfil covenants of the lease and in particular that to pay the rent. A multiple retailer or a well-established local trader with goodwill are obvious examples of good covenants. It may be thought, however, that something of a paradox is developing with the ability of relatively newly

---

*It is interesting to note, however, that under the General Development Order 1988 planning permission is no longer required for a change of use under the Use Classes Order 1987, from premises selling food and drink (class A3) to Financial and Professional Services (A2). This means that a lively restaurant/cafe frontage could become an estate agent/building society.

established concerns with newly established markets to pay the highest rents, such as specialist multiple clothes shops which spring up in prime locations all over the country. It has, however, always been recognised that trades with high profit margins such as jewellers can afford to pay high rents, and therefore perhaps the type of investment covenant created is not so new in principle. While shops in prime positions remain attractive investments, those in secondary positions are becoming less so as the general economic situation has forced the closure of some small businesses and the multiples have rationalised and consolidated in the prime positions. The exception is the demand for large out-of-town retail warehouse units for such concerns as cut-price carpet and furniture dealers.

As regards the premises themselves, the structural condition, design and shape of the shop and its facilities for loading and storage are all relevant to the valuation. Other physical features such as a forecourt (with rights to trade thereon), upper floors and basement are all factors to be considered.

Yields for freehold shops in prime positions may be around 4.5% to 5.5%, while those in secondary positions may be around 10% or more, with shades between. It should be pointed out that it is not always easy to distinguish where prime positions end and secondary positions begin in any particular town, and it may be more sensible to talk about '100% positions, 90% positions, and so on'.

Offices

The positioning of office properties is less crucial than that of shops. Offices should be located in an area served by good transport and other facilities, but the precise position within that general location is generally of less importance. The exception to this general rule relates to the small specialised areas of the City of London, which are traditionally occupied by banking, insurance and shipping agencies, where prestige and a high degree of personal contact are of importance.

As regards the letting, it is generally better to let a block as a whole, and a government department, for example, would make an ideal choice of tenant. If a property is let in suites, it has the disadvantage of creating management problems for the landlord, and the provision of services in some form or another is generally necessary. On the other hand, if the landlord is prepared for such problems of management, higher aggregate rents may be achieved in certain instances if an office property can be let in suites to, for example, legal and other professional practices. It should be borne in mind that, except in the case of building societies and estate agents who require well-placed ground-floor accommodation, tenants of office premises are less likely to build up goodwill than those of shop premises. Accordingly they are less likely to feel tied to the premises, and to this extent an office investment may be less secure than a shop.

The supply of offices is generally somewhat more elastic than that of shops. This of course is a generalisation and in the City of London for example, planning controls and physical barriers produce a relatively inelastic supply. On the other hand, office supply in the short to medium term is liable to be relatively elastic in most provincial towns.

Prime city offices may yield about 6%, with city fringes and other locations yielding in the region of 6% to 7% depending on the market. Inferior investments will of course yield more.

Industrial

Included under this heading may be hi-tech uses of a quasi-office nature as separately dealt with under the General Development Order 1988, less modern factories and warehouses built say from the 1960s onwards, and inferior old properties including multistorey factories and warehouses. More analysis of industrial investment is given in Chapter 14. It is interesting to note that under the General Development Order 1988, planning permission is no longer required for a change of use from General Industrial (B2) to Light Industrial or Business (B1). An industrial estate could therefore turn into an office campus without the need for planning permission.

Simplified planning zones (SPZs) set out by the Department of the Environment in November 1992 were intended to secure development or redevelopment and simplify the grant of planning permission for types of development specified. Conforming development does not require planning permission, thus encouraging development of large old industrial areas or new employment areas.

Accessibility to transport routes, sources of raw materials, labour and a market for the products have been the traditional factors governing the location of industry. Some of these factors are now becoming less important as the value of the product rises in relation to the value of the raw material input, and as electricity, with its large distribution network, becomes a primary source of power. It is important for factories and warehouses to be located near a good road network – in the case of perishable goods easy access to the market is still of prime importance – but on the whole industries are becoming more footloose and less tied to the traditional industrial areas. A further factor affecting location is government policy with regard to attempting to direct the location of new industrial development.

There has also been a traditional tendency for manufacturing firms to cluster by type according to their industry. This has had the advantage of attracting and developing a skilled pool of labour. It has the disadvantage, however, of vulnerability: should the whole industry run into difficulties, factories may become vacant and difficult to relet.

Old factories and warehouses frequently have the disadvantage of being situated in congested areas, with difficult vehicular access, and the physical disability of being constructed on more than one floor, with weak upper floors with poor access thereto. Modern industrial properties, on the other hand, tend to be situated on industrial estates in suburban locations having easy vehicular access. They tend to be erected on relatively large sites with adequate space for parking, loading and unloading, and providing the possibilities of future extension of the property. They are generally single-storey (possibly with mezzanine office floors), with large unobstructed spaces for modern production-line processes and adequate height for fork-lift trucks (generally 18 ft to eaves). Other normal requirements would include adequate floor loading capability (generally 500 lb/sq ft), and an average of about 10% or more of floor space devoted to ancillary offices with separate toilet facilities. Legislative requirements relating to industrial buildings include the Factory Acts and the Control of Pollution Act 1974.

As investments, industrial properties have the disadvantage of being short-lived because of the physical wear and tear they receive, and also because industrial processes tend to change over time, and design requirements change accordingly. They may also be adapted or have plant installed for a specialist process which is difficult and expensive to reinstate or remove should a re-letting become necessary. It is partly for these reasons that light industrial or warehousing and hi-tech investments are more in demand by institutional investors than heavy industrial.

This sector showed fairly poor returns in the 1980s and subsequently yields went up to around 9% to 10%. Yields are still around 10%. Yields on very old industrial investments may of course well exceed these figures.

The supply of prime industrial property is relatively more elastic in response to changes in demand compared with shops and offices. The range of locations is generally far greater than that for prime retail space and the development process is relatively fast. Again, this is of course a generalisation and the supply of industrial space in popular areas will be relatively less elastic.

Residential Property

The story of the turnabout in the proprietorship of dwellings over the last 60 years may not only seem extraordinary in itself but provides an interesting social commentary on the UK during a major part of the 20th century. Official statistics show that in 1914, 10% of dwellings were owner-occupied, with virtually the entire remaining 90% being in the hands of private landlords. In 1991 it was estimated that the figures were 68% and 7% respectively, with the remaining 25% comprising Local Authority and Housing Association rented property.

Thus the private sector has diminished dramatically, losing its proportion of the market almost equally to owner-occupiers and the new local authority rented sector. There is a negative and a positive aspect to this. The negative aspect is that as a result of the statutory control of rents, in general it no longer makes financial sense to let residential property. The positive aspect is the desire and ability of a major sector of the population to buy the dwellings they occupy, and their encouragement in this objective by successive governments in the granting of tax relief on mortgage interest for owner-occupier house purchase and the exemption from capital gains tax on sale.

A large proportion of privately-rented dwellings is still subject to the Rent Act 1977 which provides security of tenure and regulation of rents, the rateable value limits being £1,500 in London and £750 elsewhere. Under the system of regulated rents provided for by the Acts, the Rent Officer is given the theoretically impossible task of having to assess a rent on the assumption that 'scarcity' is not a factor to be considered. Various means of dealing with this problem have been tried, and gradually a pattern of established rents and methods of assessment have been built up. Currently, it would appear that the greatest discrepancy between market rents and regulated rents appears at the bottom end of the market, while at the top end there is in some cases little, if any, discrepancy. A major change in policy, however, has now taken place with regard to new lettings whereby the 'fair rent' system will no longer apply under the Housing Act 1988.

The other main areas of statutory intervention in the residential sector include the enforcement of landlord's statutory liability for repairs and the making of closing or clearance orders in relation to unfit dwellings as provided for in the Housing Acts. While on the subject of repairs, it is worth noting that a heavy repairing burden on a landlord may place the whole income in jeopardy, and could therefore be a major risk affecting yield.

The business of obtaining vacant possession has almost become a speciality for some operators, particularly the 'break-up

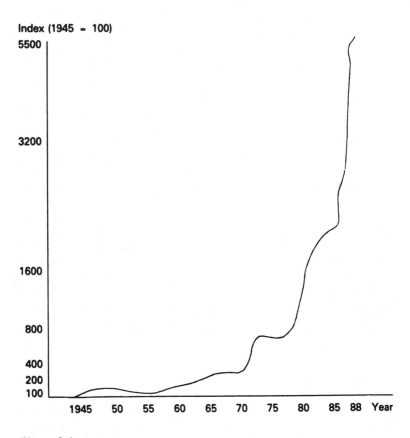

Figure 2.1

operators'. This expression is not quite as ominous as it sounds, but concerns purchasing blocks of flats which are part let, part vacant, and selling vacant units on the open market and let units to tenants. This is a high-risk, high-profit venture for the successful which is not of interest to institutional investors except for the purpose of off-loading unwanted blocks to such operators.

In the past, managing residential property in such a way as to avoid the Rent Acts was not the type of operation with which institutions would wish to involve themselves. Nor were the institutions interested in regulated tenancies with all the burdens of repair which normally go with these. The overall effect of statutory intervention is that there are two tiers of rental values and two tiers of capital value depending on whether or not the tenants are protected and their rents regulated. Because of the possibility of the rent varying and the capital value changing (due to the prospect, for example, of obtaining vacant possession), there is little consistency in the pattern of the yields. In time, if the new legislation is allowed to remain on the statute book this two-tier market may disappear. The legislation is, however, a political hot potato.

To conclude, UK investors have been dissuaded from investing in the sector because of government interference, small lot sizes and the tax attractions of owner-occupation. In the long term, owner-occupied houses have proved an extremely sound investment. For example, a limited study of a sample of approximately 80 fairly similar residential properties in the Brighton area was carried out (see Figure 2.1). This indicated an annual increase in the value of owner-occupied houses since 1945 of about 9.5%. More significantly, the annual increase since 1970 has been some 15.5%, with an approximate doubling of values between 1985 and 1988. By 1994, prices had dropped about 30% from the 1988 peak, thus revealing that in the short term, housing may not represent a sound investment. This fall in values produced the widespread phenomenon of 'negative equity' in the early 1990s, thus creating further stagnation in the market. After a decade of relatively poor performance, the owner-occupied market recovered the levels of 1988 in the late 1990s.

Agricultural Property

Yields on agricultural investments were traditionally lower than on other types of property. For various reasons, this type of investment was regarded as extremely secure. Until the 1970s and early 1980s, yields were low in the region of 3% to 5%. Recently however, there has been negative income growth and a decline of let land. The number of transactions is so low as to make any meaningful generalisation about yields difficult, although yields of as high as 10% to 11% have been recorded.[1] Values in the agricultural sectors have in recent times generally underperformed commercial property.

Special Properties

These include cinemas, hotels, petrol filling stations, public houses and others. Such properties often have a quasi-monopolist element. In the case of cinemas, for example, there may only be one in a particular town, or, in the case of a petrol filling station, its position is of such importance that two such properties may be close together, but one may be less conspicuous from the highway than the other, such that the earning potential of the two properties is totally different.

This type of property presents two difficulties. One is of valuation and the other relates to assessing its merits as an investment. This latter problem can largely be summed up thus: where a major element in the value of a property investment relates to the business acumen of the tenant, to the position of the property in relation to surrounding development over which the investor has no control, or to a current fashion in leisure activity, for example, the risks of such an investment are high.

Investment in such property therefore requires specialist advice and may be only for the specialist investor or alternatively for a very large and diversified portfolio. Problems with the valuation of hotel and restaurant investments, for instance the valuation of the Queens Moat Houses portfolio of hotels in the mid-1990s, confirm the need for specialist advice.

Development in Sectors of the Market

The established classification of property investments changed in the 1980s with the addition of hi-tech developments, retail warehouses, retail parks, mixed used developments and speciality shops. Workshop conversions with residential or studio space also created an innovative sub-sector. Some of these new categories were encouraged by the changes in the planning controls. The Town and Country Planning Use Classes Order 1987 lists the categories of property use and within each classification it is possible to change use without any additional planning consent. This legislation established the Class B1 which is a business class allowing movement across the divide from light industrial use to office use. This change caused a remarkable shake-up in the office sector but even more so in the industrial sector. Business space became a recognised sector of the investment market dealing with B1 properties. In addition, the concept of business parks was established as opposed to dealing with a block of offices or an industrial estate. The legislation allowed this change of use within the band of uses as long as substantial external physical alterations were not required. However, any change of use which required movement between one class and another required specific consent. Class B1, as well as combining office use with light industrial use, also generally indicated a hi-tech usage or specification to the building.

Additional developments in industrial space saw the use of retail warehouses, a retail outlet forming part of a warehouse facility. These retail outlets were either a small part of existing business activity, like a trade counter, or the main activity as with a DIY store or furniture warehouse. With retail warehousing, the location and structure of the building is related to the warehousing sector but the economic analysis and financial appraisal used in such developments relates more to the retail sector. The leisure industry has also followed this trend with 'leisure boxes' enabling flexible use of the facilities. 'Dinosaur World' near Newhaven is an example of a warehouse accommodating a plant nursery and garden centre being extended to include a Dinosaur museum, an extensive botanical garden, a miniature village and amusements.

References

1 Country Practitioner: 'Investment – a curate's egg', 8821EG62.

General References

Bowie, N. 'Depreciation: Who Hoodwinked Whom?' *Estates Gazette*, May 1 1982, pp. 405–11.
Fraser, W. 'Rates Reform and the Value of Investment Property', 274EG990.
Mortimer, E. and Edwards, M. 'B2 change raise, industrial pressure', *Estates Times*, November 25 1988.

Chapter Three

Determinants of Value

Supply and Demand

In elementary economic terms, price is determined by the forces of supply and demand, and as noted in the previous chapter, the supply of property is relatively inelastic due to a number of factors including the physical nature of land itself, the planning laws and security of tenure.

The demand for property is also relatively inelastic – the basic need for living accommodation provides the obvious example – but again there are many factors which affect demand and the degree of inelasticity of that demand. Before proceeding to examine these factors, it would be as well to confirm that it is effective demand which is being considered; in other words the purchaser must be able to translate the demand into actual purchase by being in possession of the necessary funds or have the income or potential income to command a sufficient loan to provide him with them.

Demand is of many kinds. Potential purchasers have different motives for acquiring property. There are four major categories of motive, sometimes found in combination with one another. These are: (i) for occupation; (ii) for investment – generally long-term; (iii) for speculation – generally short-term; and (iv) for development. In every case the purchaser hopes to receive benefits from his acquisition, either financial benefits or benefits in kind arising from occupation. It is the valuation of these benefits by potential purchasers which will be reflected in the price or annual rent bid for the property.

Some of the main factors affecting demand are outlined below:

(i)   The state of the general economy – in a recession, business-people will postpone investment and householders will be fearful of moving 'up-market', and the reverse conditions will apply in a boom.

(ii)   Changes in the structure of the economy and the organisation
       of businesses. For example, the long-term trend from
       manufacturing to service industry has increased the demand
       for offices to rent *vis-à-vis* factories. The move toward home
       working or teleworking (working from home using computer
       links) and more efficient use of space, may in time decrease
       office demand.

(iii) Abnormal increases in cost of ownership or occupancy other
       than rent. In arguing against a proposed increase in rent, a
       business tenant may examine the revenue of his business and
       also the outgoings such as rates, costs-in-use of the building
       (heating, lighting, cleaning etc), costs of insurance and repair,
       and the costs of operating his business. If he finds that
       outgoings are rising faster than revenue, it may be that rent,
       being perhaps more negotiable than some of the other
       outgoings, forms a residual in his calculation of profitability
       and of necessity becomes proportionately smaller. If this
       pattern becomes general among business tenants, then it may,
       sooner or later, become reflected in market rents. Some argued
       that this theory was borne out by the fact that rates as a
       percentage of rents increased from 11% in 1970 to 70% in 1976
       in the case of City of London offices and that over the latter
       part of this period when increases were at their greatest there
       were reductions in rent of up to 50% between 1973 and 1976.
       Although there were many other factors affecting the boom
       and slump of the mid-1970s which are examined later, it was
       seriously argued in 1977 that the level of rates was such as to
       reduce the rent bid of tenants and aspiring tenants. It may not
       of course always be possible for a tenant to shift the burden of
       increased rates to the landlord as landlords may prefer to
       leave property vacant rather than accept reduced rents and
       rents on review will of course not normally come down due to
       the practice of upwards only rent review clauses. Conversely,
       a Landlord may not necessarily benefit by a reduction in rates
       in the form of increased rents. The latter will depend to some
       extent upon the elasticity of supply of the type of property
       concerned. In the case of industrial property for example,
       which has a relative elasticity of supply, a rise in demand
       resulting from a decrease in rates is more likely to lead to an
       increase in supply than an increase of rent in the short to
       medium term.[1] Costs-in-use are dealt with in a little more
       detail in the next section. In most centres, office rates and
       other costs of occupancy have continued to increase faster
       than rental values.

(iv)   The productivity of the property. This factor reduces to the
       simple proposition that the more per square metre which a

commercial property can earn for its occupier, the more he will be prepared to pay in rent. Thus well-located offices command higher rentals than factories, and this is not solely a determinant of the costs of producing these buildings.

(v) Government intervention. This has already been dealt with in detail, but it is relevant in the present context to illustrate by example some of its effects on demand. Grand-aided schemes such as are available in the regions of high unemployment will be considered by a businessperson in determining the rent he can afford to pay in various regions of the UK. Variations in taxes are another factor.

(vi) Change in transport facilities. New roads may open up new commuting possibilities thereby increasing the demand for business premises in a town and the demand for housing in its newly served environs.

(vii) Alterations in the size and structure of the population. Thus, for example, an increase in the number of old people will lead to increased demand for land uses related to this change, such as sheltered housing, hospitals, and so on.

(viii) Alterations in the cost of borrowing.

(ix) Variations in the amount of money which lenders are prepared to lend.

Costs-in-Use

The total costs of a building consist of the capital cost and the costs-in-use (operating costs and maintenance costs). In the past, developers have been mainly concerned with minimising capital costs at the possible expense of operating and maintenance costs. With the current high costs of maintenance and the realisation that the cost of heating, lighting and ventilating may amount to as much as 30 to 40% of rental value, prospective purchasers and tenants of such buildings are taking greater account of maintenance and operating costs, with a consequential effect on capital and rental values.

From the investor's point of view, costs-in-use are therefore important mainly for two reasons. Firstly, high cost-in-use may result in correspondingly low rental values as tenants' valuers try to forecast the service charge over the term of the lease and negotiate accordingly. Secondly, landlords are frequently responsible for maintaining and operating vacant or part-vacant buildings.

It is possible at the design stage to evaluate the total cost of alternative designs by converting all costs, including future costs-in-use, to a net present value, or alternatively by converting all costs, including initial capital cost, to an equivalent annual value.

Costs-in-use appraisals may also take account of such factors as taxation and investment allowances, and replacement services.

Market Value

Having in this chapter and the previous one examined the economic forces of supply and demand which determine price, it is now proposed to look a little more closely at the concept of price and how this relates to market value.

In normal circumstances one would expect price to equate to market value, but this is not always the case, and it is therefore necessary to define precisely what is meant by market value. 'Open market value' is defined by the Royal Institution of Chartered Surveyors[2] in the following terms:

'The best price at which an interest in a property might reasonably be expected to be sold by private treaty at the date of valuation, assuming:

(a) a willing seller;
(b) a reasonable period within which to negotiate the sale, taking into account the nature of the property and the state of the market;
(c) values will remain static throughout the period;
(d) the property will be freely exposed to the market;
(e) no account is to be taken of an additional bid by a special purchaser.'

Each of these assumptions will now be briefly examined.

(a) A Willing Seller

This would not include a sale due to harassment or under the shadow of compulsory purchase, liquidation or bankruptcy. Although acquiring authorities and Receivers in Bankruptcy have statutory guidelines on valuation, such transactions are not normally regarded as good evidence of market value.

(b) A Reasonable Period to Negotiate the Sale

Such an assumption would again rule out the forced sale situation where the vendor has imposed a time-limit for completion which cannot be regarded as a reasonable period.

(c) Values will Remain Static Throughout the Period

This relates to the period which inevitably arises between the point in time at which a deal is struck and the date upon which the contract of sale is signed, or legal completion takes place.

In entering a boom or slump, market conditions can change very quickly – too quickly in fact for the legal and other processes necessary to conclude the transaction. It is under these conditions that charges of 'gazumping' or 'reverse gazumping' are raised or it may be that the parties to the transaction stand by the original deal and are prepared to conclude the transaction at a price which at that time does not equate to market value.

(d) The Property will be Freely Exposed to the Market

It is obviously important for potential purchasers to have knowledge of the existence and nature of available property, such as through advertising in the local newspapers and professional press, estate agents window displays and boards etc.

(e) No Account to be Taken of a Special Purchaser's Bid

Special purchasers are those who are prepared to pay over the market value for some reason, such as a tenant in occupation who may be prepared to pay more for the superior interest than would a normal investor, or a farmer who is prepared to pay more than anyone else for an adjoining holding to make his own more viable. Another possible class of special purchaser is the retailer prepared to pay *key money* to be represented in a centre. Key money may be defined as that part of the capital price obtained for the lease of a shop which is additional to the sum of the capitalised value of the estimated profit rental and of the value of any shop fittings of general use to an ingoing occupier. The key money element in shop prices tends to be volatile. The term also applies to certain payments unlawfully demanded of incoming tenants by outgoing tenants or landlords of residential property protected by the Rent Acts.[3] It is debatable, however, whether this is a true special purchaser or whether the key money is in fact an element in market value. The whole assumption relating to special purchaser is in fact contentious. If the obvious and only purchaser for a property is the special purchaser, then does this not constitute the market, albeit a market of one? This may be a matter of semantics, but it would be as well for a valuer advising on this situation to draw his client's attention to the special purchaser bid, even if for asset valuation purposes, at any rate, it is excluded from the market valuation.

A revised definition came into effect from June 1 1992. The principal change is that the 'reasonable period' for marketing the interest is now assumed to have taken place before the valuation date which in turn is assumed to coincide with the date of completion of the sale. To meet the point that, in practice, a purchase price is usually fixed, not on the date of completion of the sale but on an earlier date when unconditional contracts were exchanged, the valuer is required to assume that circumstances, values and market conditions at the date of contract were the same as those prevailing at the date of completion (ie the date of valuation). Thus there can no longer be an assumed marketing period following the date of valuation and so the provision that 'values will remain static' disappears. The 'reasonable period' in normal circumstances should not exceed a few months. The sale of an interest is assumed to have been completed unconditionally for a cash consideration. The valuer may not assume deferred completion, stage payments or consideration in terms of shares or an exchange of land. 'Proper marketing' means the most appropriate method to effect a disposal at the best price.[4]

Other instances of 'wrong' prices being paid could arise from mistakes or inexperience on the part of the purchaser or vendor, and such 'fluke transactions' if spotted, should clearly be disregarded as not providing evidence of market value.

Equating price with market value is partly connected with the process of ironing out the imperfections in the property market, and it is therefore convenient in this context to deal with two topics relevant to this process, viz professional advice and property market information.

The *professions of the land* have a major role to play in ironing out imperfections in the market. Inadequate knowledge on the part of individuals regarding the physical and legal features of a property and their effect on value can be overcome by employing a professional valuer. Professional valuers will have the knowledge and expertise, through the various established methods of valuation, to make a valuation even in the absence of transaction evidence. The valuer will know the best means of obtaining information to assist in the valuation, and be conversant with the statutory rules which need to be applied in making certain valuations.

The role of valuer is often, but not always, combined with that of estate agent and/or estate manager. Estate agents may be said to be the catalysts of the market. Without them it is difficult to see how a property market as we know it could exist. They are localised, and they are open to the casual caller. Hence individuals who have not yet formulated firm plans about their intentions or requirements with regard to property can obtain the benefit of the estate agent's knowledge and advice of local or specialised market conditions. Agents may therefore be instrumental in crystallising the ideas of individuals in this connection and then matching the requirements of prospective vendors to those of prospective purchasers.

The management role of many agents is also important. The knowledge which can be obtained from management records regarding the level of rents and outgoings such as repairs is very important when it comes to advising clients concerning prospective transactions in property investments. The knowledge and information which agents are often able to obtain and pass on to clients may frequently be extended through the contacts they acquire with other people in the property business. A more formal means of co-operation may exist through agents combining together for joint listing and advertising of properties.

Agents, and qualified agents in particular, may be able to give specialised advice with regard to such matters as valuation, statutory planning and building controls, advice on building costs and so on. The major asset of estate agents must be, however, their marketing ability. They are able to offer advice and to undertake the best means of advertising, mode of sale and any necessary negotiations.

As regards *property market information*, this is important in enabling putative purchasers and their professional advisers to make the necessary comparisons in order to reach proper opinions.

The prices of most investments are monitored daily by the Stock Exchange information system, the financial press, official bulletins and other media. Because of its heterogeneous nature this is not and cannot be the case with property. If deals are struck privately, then information is not usually released. If properties are sold at auction, then the price is public knowledge, but without detailed information about the property concerned, the bare bones of a deal may or may not be of substantial use to valuers and others who are interested.

There are various sources of property market information. Firstly, estate agents and managers keep records of transactions for future use. Secondly, details of deals and auctions sometimes appear in the press – the local press and the property journals in particular. Background information about the market may also be obtained from the financial and economic press. Thirdly, the major firms of estate agents produce reports on the state of the market or of the sub-sectors with which they are concerned.

A certain amount of information useful to valuers may be gleaned from various public sources. These include local authorities, which are obliged to keep open for public inspection a register of planning applications and records of council and certain committee decisions in that regard, the Development Plan, and the valuation list, containing a record of all rateable values in the district. Rent Officers also keep open to inspection details of registered rents. More general information concerning trends in agricultural property is also available from the relevant government departments. Reference may also be made to the construction and cost-of-living indices for background information.

On the subject of available information, Inland Revenue District Valuers are at something of an advantage, it being part of the conveyancing process to submit to the District Valuer particulars of all transactions (both private and public). This information is being made available in one form or another to private practitioners but the problem of retaining confidentiality of the parties involved in the transaction may be insuperable. Inland Revenue information, however, is made available in a generalised form in the Property Market Report. There has been much debate on the release of information in the market. Information will improve the quality of valuations, but in some situations in a falling market, landlords will attempt to conceal low rent agreements by confidentiality clauses in leases and by various incentives such as rent-free periods, phased initial rents and contributions to fitting-out costs.

Other Types of Value

Market value, although the most objective means of measuring value, is not the only one. Individuals may make higher subjective valuations in particular cases than would be reflected in market opinion for social or aesthetic reasons or for the fact that the 'value in use' to them of the property is different from the market value. The additional benefit over and above market value which a purchaser will obtain is, in economic terms known as a *consumer surplus*. Market circumstances may persuade buyers to bid away some or all of their consumer surplus with resultant price increases. Studies have shown, for example, that an individual householder's preference for not moving house may cause him to be unwilling to accept the market price for his house if offered it. In fact, he may require considerably more to induce him to overcome his inertia. Likewise a property investor may prefer to retain a property rather than sell it at market value because of the capital gains tax he would incur on sale.

Occupiers of property are also frequently known to have works of adaptation carried out which cost more than the addition to value which they create. This may be due to idiosyncratic preferences or to the needs of a particular business or manufacturing process being carried out on the property. Another area of subjective valuation arises in the case of public development, where non-commercial criteria must sometimes be adopted for the benefit or needs of the community or a particular section thereof.

It is with market value that this work is primarily concerned, although a return will be made to the concept of subjective value, particularly in the context of the individual investor's tax position.

The Distinction between Valuation and Analysis

The property crash in the early 1970s focused attention on valuation methods used in the profession. Over the period since then there have been a number of pressures on valuation professionals to improve the quality and standard of the valuations produced. This has arisen for a number of reasons. Large-scale investment, for instance, has taken place in recent years and the investment advisers acting for the institutions and investors are looking for more analysis in the valuations which have been carried out. Because of situations which have occurred in the past involving institutional investors, where actual returns on property investments have not reflected target returns set out in accordance with the price paid, there has been much debate about the validity of the methods used. There is also much more awareness in the market now, in terms of the responsibilities of the professional to clients' demands, that the property professional should not just act as an agent but provide during the buying and selling process some idea to the client of the forecast of income arising from the investment in the future.

This added awareness and monitoring of valuation procedures has been a subject of debate in the professional institutions as well as in the market-place. Suggestions by leading members of the RICS are that valuations should try to reflect a view of the future movement of prices and forecast potential supply and demand situations which may affect price levels. The findings of the Mallinson Report suggest that the valuer should get clearer instructions from the client and should more clearly explain the valuation of property in company accounts. In addition, the report suggests that there should be more comment on valuation risk factors, price trends and economic factors and the use of more refined discounted cashflow techniques. This debate and earlier debates have combined to demand that, in what has previously been called property valuation, a more extensive service of property analysis be provided. Generally, the approach that should be taken (see Baum and Crosby[5]) is that the overall property appraisal should be clearly divided between property valuation for purchase, that is the valuation for market price and the subsequent analysis of performance. In the first case, this is defined as valuation and in the second case it is defined as analysis, while the overall process is generally termed 'property appraisal'. Thus the valuation of a property, that is the calculation of the exchange value of property, is different from the subsequent analysis of the performance of the investment which is the appraisal of its actual worth. Calculations before and after purchase will not agree because of the lack of perfect knowledge in the market at the time of the transaction and the inability to predict future changes in the cash flow and the risk profile of the investment accurately. Thus the techniques discussed later on in this book can be used to anticipate the market value or else to record and analyse the progress of the investment subsequent to purchase. However, it is still important to understand the difference between these two approaches.

Property Cycles

The property industry shows a cycle of activity that reflects the general business cycle. This problem, relating to changes in the returns in the market and having a dramatic effect on investment and development activity in the market, is especially evident in the office sector. Recent research by the Royal Institution of Chartered Surveyors[6] provided some insights into the operation of this cycle. The research looked at the structure of the property industry and found that there were a number of interest groups operating in the market; namely, occupiers, investors and developers. For occupiers, property was an input to their production process, a factor of production for their goods and services. For investors, it provided an asset on which returns would be generated and compared to other asset classes and, for developers, property was the output of their production process. The interaction between these groups provides the indications of how the market operates. In the research, property cycles were defined as recurrent but irregular fluctuations in the rate of all-property total returns. Aggregate property returns were chosen to show the cyclical patterns and rental performance; yield movements and development activities are linked to the property cycle but these linkages are elastic and flexible. Property cycles were found to be of four to five years' duration and these cycles matched the general business cycle in the economy. The causes of the cycle were twofold:

(i)   causes external to the property industry
(ii) causes internal to the property industry.

External influences in the occupier markets including cyclical demand factors, GDP, consumer spending, financial and business services' demand and manufacturing demand act as the prime influences on rental values, interest rates and inflation. In the investment markets, the external drivers are bond yields and inflation which have a significant influence on property yields and property investment by UK financial institutions. The internal influences or drivers are the development cycle, the development lag (caused by the inflexibility in the building stock) and rent. Development activity showed internal cyclical supply patterns without even considering the external demand factors.

The formal findings of the survey were that:

(i)   the UK property industry shows a recurrent cycle which meets the qualitative definition applied to economic cycles but cannot be described definitively by statistical techniques;
(ii) the property cycle is the compounded result of cyclical influence from the wider economy, which is coupled with cyclical tendencies that are inherent in the property market;
(iii) the critical linkages between property cycles and economic cycles can be captured in simple models.

Further research is thus required into the external and internal drivers to discover whether this impact can be smoothed, thus taking away the excesses of the cycle. The property market has integrated with the financial sector and there are wider implications to a market collapse in the sector; in the 1974 collapse it was secondary banks which were involved, but now there is much greater bank involvement. The damage that can be done to the financial system in the event of a collapse will be more general, the so-called contagion effect. The property cycle is related to the business cycle and this can be seen as a series of fluctuations in activity that proceed in an irregular way: depression (low level of consumer demand and economic activity), recovery, boom (industry fully productive), recession and so on.[7]

References

1 Fraser, W. 'Rates Reform and the Value of Investment Property', 274EG990.
2 RICS Guidance Notes on the Valuation of Assets.
3 *The Glossary of Property Terms*, Estates Gazette, 1989.
4 Beaman, M. *Open Market Value Redefined*, General Practice Information Service, RICS, May 1992.
5 Baum, A. and Crosby, N. *Property Investment Appraisal*, Routledge, 1988.
6 'Property cycles explained', *Estates Gazette*, November 25 1995, pp. 147–8.
7 Royal Institution of Chartered Surveyors, *Understanding the Property Cycle: Economic Cycles and Property Cycles*, RICS, May 1994.

Lease Terms

The terms under which a property is let or is likely to be let are of prime importance in an investment valuation. Fortunately for the valuer, leases of commercial property are tending to become more standardised. Perhaps, however, that is all the more reason for the valuer to be on his guard for the unusual covenant which could materially affect the value of the property.

If the valuer is involved in the creation of the investment, his main duties would consist of negotiating the terms and communicating them to the solicitor. Apart from the rent and other major terms he may have to negotiate comparatively detailed matters. This is because the rent agreed is only agreed as part of a 'package deal' of other terms and conditions.

One particular point which should be considered at this stage is whether or not a rent-free period for 'fitting out' is to be allowed. Other points which must be settled before the lease is signed – preferably well before – is the need for the prospective tenant to provide references and/or guarantors. These matters will of course depend upon the known status of the prospective tenant.

The usual modern commercial lease is a 'full repairing and insuring lease' (*FRI lease*) under which the tenant is responsible for all outgoings. It is this type of lease which generally forms the basis of the lease terms set out below. These terms are not intended to be definitive. Not all the covenants and terms specified will be relevant in every case, and many matters of detail primarily the concern of the solicitor are omitted. Alongside some of the terms there are notes on points of valuation, negotiation or management.

The Essentials

The following terms are essential to the creation of a lease and normally precede landlord's and tenant's covenants:

(i)   The parties to the agreement.
(ii) Description of the property. This should be precise and, if possible, accompanied by a plan. It should include all ancillary rights and easements such as access, car-parking, and drainage rights, and it should reserve to the landlord any necessary rights and easements he needs for the benefit of retained land.
(iii) Duration of the lease and the commencing date. In deciding the term he can offer, the landlord should consider the timing of future redevelopment, if any, and the desirability or otherwise of leases falling in together in the case of multi-let property. As regards the latter, when future redevelopment prospects exist, this is obviously desirable, and it can also be more convenient from a management point of view. Against this must be balanced the risk of a number of voids occurring simultaneously. In considering the duration of the lease, the tenant will need to have regard to any improvements he intends to carry out.
(iv) The rent. Apart from the amount of rent, the timing of payment should be specified. Quarterly in advance is now normal. A simple rent review provision could be incorporated at this stage, but a more complex one should be set out as a separate item (see on).

Tenant's Covenants

(i)   To pay the rent. This may include a covenant to pay interest on arrears.
(ii) To insure against fire and possibly storm and tempest to the full value of the premises in the joint names of the landlord and tenant. More likely, however, the landlord will insure recouping the premium from the tenant.
(iii) To pay tenant's outgoings, including rates and taxes.
(iv) To comply with various statutory requirements. These may be spelt out according to the circumstances, and may include the need for the tenant to obtain any necessary licence to operate his business.
(v)   To repair. Exceptionally or in the case of multi-let properties, the landlord may undertake to repair or to share the burden with the tenant. In the case of external and structural repairs to a multi-let property the landlord may arrange to recoup the cost from the tenants, apportioning according to area

occupied or some other formula. A specific dilapidations clause requiring the tenant to make good any dilapidations on expiry may also be included.

The Landlord and Tenant Act 1927 limits the damage recoverable by a landlord in respect of a breach of the tenant's covenant to repair. The Act provides the tenant with two arguments to limit the landlord's claim for damages:

(1) that there has been no diminution in the value of the reversion;
(2) works of repair will be overtaken by demolition or alteration of the building.

Both arguments were used in *Ultraworth Ltd* v *General Accident Fire and Life Assurance Corporation plc* [2000] EGCS 19.[1]

Recent cases in this area have included circumstances where a landlord's right to enter and carry out repairs at the tenant's cost will be denied (*London Borough of Hammersmith* v *Creska Ltd* [1999]) and another case which limited the ability of landlords to carry out repairs and recover the cost by way of a service charge (*Scottish Mutual Assurance plc* v *Jardine Public Relations Ltd* [1999] EGCS 43).[2]

(vi) To paint the property. The tenant may be required to paint externally at stated intervals, and also possibly to redecorate internally at stated intervals.

(vii) To pay a service charge. This is, of course, linked to a corresponding landlord's covenant to provide services. This is a complex subject and problems commonly arise unless full details are set out in the lease document. Such problems might include a dispute over the exact nature of the services to be provided and the method of calculating the service charge. These points are dealt with under the subject of outgoings in the next chapter.

(viii) To yield up possession at the end of the lease. In practice, business tenants are protected by the Landlord and Tenant Act 1954 unless the landlord has one of the statutory grounds for obtaining possession. One of these grounds is a proposal to redevelop. This must be a firm proposal (Landlord & Tenant Act 1954 Section 30(i)(f)). Note, however, the case of *Esselte AB* v *Pearl Assurance plc* [1997] 1 EGLR 73, which found that if the tenant is not in occupation when the contractual term expires, the 1954 Act will not apply to the lease.[3]

(ix) Not to do anything to render the insurance policy invalid. In addition there are likely to be one or two other clauses relating to insurance – the treatment of claims etc.

(x) Not to make alterations. As with services, this is a complex item which needs a good deal of attention.

As regards any improvements, in the case of business tenancies, the Landlord and Tenant Act 1927 prevents the charging of a premium on the carrying out of tenant's improvements. It should be noted that even in the event of an absolute prohibition being placed in the lease, the law implies that the landlord's consent should not be unreasonably withheld, and the Landlord and Tenant Act 1927 may specifically allow the tenant to carry out improvements despite an express covenant to the contrary.

Finally on this subject, it may be desirable to require the tenant to remove additional structures on the expiration of the lease, as, for example, low quality partitioning which is likely to damage the landlord's reversion.

(xi)   Not to use the premises for a specified range of purposes, or, contrarily, positively to use for certain purposes. The inability to move outside a narrowly defined category of use may affect the tenant's ability to assign the property and hence its lettability and possibly the level of rental obtainable. In the case of a shopping centre, however, from the landlord's point of view, and also from that of the majority of tenants in the long run, such covenants are usually essential to its proper planning and management. They may also be applied in certain other instances, as for example in the case of specialised office use such as banking in multi-let property. Again the implied covenant regarding landlord's consent not to be unreasonably withheld applies.

(xii) Not to display advertisements without the landlord's consent.

(xiii) To obtain the landlord's consent to an assignment, such consent not to be unreasonably withheld. This is a conventional wording and there is likely to be strong tenant-resistance to attempts to impose a less generous covenant. It may be reasonable that the covenant should place an absolute prohibition on part assignments or underlettings, and on underlettings at less than a rack rent, as the latter could damage the landlord's interest on default of the head lessee. Once again the law provides an implication that the landlord's consent is not to be unreasonably withheld. It is now becoming increasingly common for landlords to require tenants to offer to surrender their leases should they wish to assign. This surrender is to be at no cost to the landlord.

This area has now been revised by the Landlord and Tenant Act 1988 which prevents landlords delaying consent. Before 1996 it was not possible for the landlord to dictate the grounds for withholding consent. The Landlord and Tenant (Covenants) Act 1995 changed this. In practice, it is usual that a landlord may reasonably withhold consent if:

- the assignee does not have the appropriate financial strength and reputation;
- the assignee is a member of the same group of companies as the tenant;
- the tenant does not agree to enter into an authorised guarantee agreement (AGA).[4]

Prior to 1996, the original tenant and each successive assignee usually agreed to accept liability for the remainder of the term. After the 1995 Act, each tenant is only responsible while a tenant. The landlord may, if it is reasonable, require a tenant to guarantee his immediate successor under an authorised guarantee agreement. The imposition and its reasonableness was consolidated in the case of *Wallis Fashion Group Ltd* v *CGU Life Assurance Ltd* [2000] 27 EG 145.[5]

Landlord's Covenants

This is normally quite a short section of the lease. Many of the points, relating to services, insurances and so on, have been dealt with above. The only remaining covenant which the landlord normally provides is the standard covenant for quiet enjoyment – meaning peaceable rather than free from noise.

Breach of a covenant for quiet enjoyment is often confused with derogation from grant. The former refers to the quality of the enjoyment of possession (*Jenkins* v *Jackson* [1988] 40 ChD 71). The latter is to do with the issue that if a person confers a particular benefit on another, he/she must not do anything which substantially deprives the other of the enjoyment of that benefit (*Moulton Building Ltd* v *City of Westminster* [1995] 30 P&CR 182).[6]

Other Points on Leases

Other terms may include:

(i) An option to break the lease. This is now rather unusual unless the landlord requires one for redevelopment purposes. The Court may not always grant such a request on a lease renewal (see *J.H. Edwards & Sons Ltd* v *Central London Commercial Estates Ltd* [1984] 2 EGLR 103). To conclude, if there are express time-limits for service of a notice to exercise a break, these must be strictly observed (*United Scientific Holdings* v *Burnley Corporation* [1977] 2 EGLR 61, although the case of *Mannai Investment Co Ltd* v *Eagle Star Life Assurance Co Ltd* [1977] 1 EGLR 57, held a notice containing a break date that was one day early to be valid.[7]

(ii) Provision for which party is to pay the legal costs associated with the lease.

(iii) Provision for rent review (see following section).

(iv) Provision for arbitration on dispute over lease terms.

(v) Proviso for re-entry on breach of covenant. In valuing a leasehold interest, particularly for mortgage purposes, special consideration needs to be given to such a provision.

(vi) Proviso for cessor of rent in the event of damage by fire.

(vii) Miscellaneous and special conditions. A number of conditions not normally incorporated may be appropriate in the case of special properties. A petrol filling station lease, for example, may provide for re-entry if the tenant does not achieve a certain level of sales, as the rent may be linked to turnover.

Reference has already been made to certain relevant statutory provisions, but the statutory modifications of covenants, particularly in the context of the Landlord and Tenant Acts 1927 and 1954, need constant attention.

One final point in this general section on lease terms concerns the case of exceptionally long leases. It may be good practice to incorporate arrangements for possible future changes in letting practice. This might relate, for example, to the calculation and frequency of rent reviews.

Rent Reviews

Until the 1950s, inflation was not considered to be a particular problem for landlords. The rent would be fixed for the term of the lease and this would be accepted by both parties as the normal basis of letting. In the inter-war period, for example, such terms could even be of considerable benefit to landlords.

With the gradual realisation that inflation was here to stay and that the rate of inflation was rising, rent reviews began to be included in long leases in the 1950s at say 21-year or 33-year intervals. In the 1960s the practice of reviewing rents of 14- or 21-year leases at seven-year intervals became the norm, and in the 1970s the five-year review and the corresponding 20-year or 25-year lease were developed. Leases of small properties to secondary tenants are often granted subject to three-year reviews or even on an annual basis.

In the early days of rent reviews, other methods of hedging the landlord's income against inflation were the granting of short leases – but this provided a greater risk of voids than with long leases – and rent increases of pre-determined amounts. This latter method was a gamble on both sides in trying to forecast the rise in property rents. If the forecast proved low the tenant benefited and on the contrary if rental levels in the market did not rise to the pre-determined level the landlord benefited. Such methods of review are still occasionally found, but the normal basis of review is to increase the rent to the full market rent. The lack of certainty about this type of provision initially caused lawyers problems in drafting suitable clauses. In an effort to make the clauses watertight the drafting has now in some cases become exceedingly complex. In essence, however, there are three basic factors which need to be covered by the clause, and these are:

(i) The machinery for effecting the rent review.
(ii) The basis of valuation including the factors to be taken into account and the assumptions to be made.
(iii) The means of settling disputes where the parties cannot agree on the revised rent.

Market conditions will affect the negotiating strengths of landlord and tenant respectively. In a landlord's letting market an 'upwards only' review may be appropriate but in a depressed market an 'upwards or downwards' clause may be negotiated by the tenant. Despite the recent recession the latter is still unusual. The upwards only provision may also include a clause requiring that immediately on the review date the rent is raised to a predetermined amount (say 30% above the existing rent) until the review is settled by agreement or arbitration. The difference between the predetermined increase and the finally agreed or settled increase would be back dated to the rent review by an appropriate adjustment.

The RICS and the Law Society produced a recommended standard basis for drafting rent reviews.[8] This recognised the need for flexibility due to special circumstances and varying market conditions, and hence provided alternative clauses to be incorporated depending on the terms negotiated, including the alternative of 'upwards only' or 'upwards and downwards' provisions. Two Model Rent Review Clauses were subsequently proposed by the Incorporated Society of Valuers and Auctioneers.[9] One of these clauses related to tenant's improvements and the other to the difficulty of assessing a ground rent in view of the likely absence of comparable lettings. The proposal was to take as a rent a percentage of the sale price of the premises with vacant possession at the valuation date.

Considered in some detail below are the three basic factors referred to earlier which need to be covered by a rent review clause.

(i) The Machinery for Effecting the Review

The usual procedure is for the landlord to propose a revised rent by a certain date, and for the tenant to be given a certain period within which to object. Negotiations will then proceed. If either party fails to adhere to the required timetable, the effects are potentially very serious. For example, a landlord could miss a review altogether, or the tenant, failing to object in time, could be stuck with the rent proposed by the landlord. The results of failure to observe the timetable will depend upon the exact wording of the lease and the surrounding circumstances, but, as a general rule now, time is generally no longer of the essence of the contract. This results from the decision in *United Scientific Holdings Ltd* v *Burnley Borough Council* [1977] 2 EGLR 61; in which Lord Diplock said:

> 'So upon the question of principle which these two appeals were brought to settle, I would hold that in the absence of any contraindications in the express words of the lease or in the interrelations of the rent review clause itself and other clauses or in the surrounding circumstances the presumption is that the timetable specified in a rent review clause for completion of the various steps for determining the rent payable in respect of the period following the review date is not of the essence of contract'.

The trend in decisions since *United Scientific Holdings* is that where time is not of the essence, mere delay, however lengthy, does not lead to a loss of the landlord's rights. To lose his rights, the landlord must have engaged in conduct or words amounting to an estoppel. (NB: The same liberal attitude towards timetable provisions does not apply, however, with regard to break clauses. The Courts have held that time is impliedly made of the essence for a rent review if the timetabling of the review machinery is closely linked to that for the option to break.)

Lord Salmon went on to add:

> 'I certainly agree that if the lessors had been guilty of unreasonable delay which had caused prejudice or hardship to the lessees they would have forfeited their rights'.

A delay of 18 months in itself was not regarded as unreasonable in *H. West & Son Ltd* v *Brech* [1982] 1 EGLR 113. Service of a trigger notice six years late however was held to be unreasonable in *Telegraph Properties (Securities) Ltd* v *Courtaulds Ltd* [1981] 1 EGLR 104.

The RICS/Law Society model clause did not make time of the essence. Mere human error in failing to observe a timetable will not normally now have disastrous consequences.

Trigger notices often state the wrong review date. The test here is whether the notice is sufficiently clear to the reasonable recipient (*Mannai Investment Co* v *Eagle Star Life Assurance Co* [1997] 1 EGLR 57.

(ii) The Basis of Valuation

Variations in leases in describing the type of rent to be determined have included such adjectives as 'fair', 'reasonable', 'commercial', 'full' and so on. The RICS/Law Society working party came to the conclusion that 'open market rent' was the best description. This in itself, however, does not provide sufficient information for the valuer to work on in arriving at a rent. There are many factors to be taken into account and assumptions to be made, and the following are the main ones which should be provided for in the lease.

(a) *The unexpired term of the lease.* There are two common variations; either that the term of the lease left at review is to be assumed to correspond to the original term of the lease, or that it is to correspond to the actual unexpired term. The RICS model clause followed the former basis on the grounds that comparable open market rents will be derived from 'full length' leases and not short unexpired terms, and that the latter basis could produce an unrealistic level of rent. In *Pivot Properties Ltd v Secretary of State for the Environment* [1980] 2 EGLR 126, the rent was to be determined on the basis of an unexpired term of five and a half years. The arbitrator determined that this was considerably lower than would be the case were it possible to import an assumption of a possible further statutory lease under the Landlord and Tenant Act 1954, and the Court held that it was possible to make this assumption.

(b) *The user clause.* There is a dilemma for a landlord in that if in the interests of good estate management he incorporates a tight user clause then this may reduce the rent obtainable on review. In *Plinth Property Investments Ltd v Mott, Hay & Anderson* [1979] 1 EGLR 17, a restriction on offices to use by consulting engineers had a depressing effect on rental value, and it was held that the landlord could not argue that he would have consented to such a change – the tenant had not applied for it. The lease may provide for the valuer to assume a wider user clause than actually exists in the lease.

(c) *The effect of tenant's improvements.* It is accepted as equitable that if a tenant makes improvements himself then the increase in rental value arising from these should be left out of account on a subsequent rent review. Otherwise the tenant will pay for them twice – once in the cost of the works and once on the increase in rent. This is, however, precisely what did happen to the unfortunate tenant in *Ponsford v HMS (Aerosols) Ltd* [1978] 2 EGLR 81, in which a 'reasonable rent' had to be determined and where the lease made no provision for excluding the rental effect of tenant's improvements. This is generally not thought to be a satisfactory result, and the RICS/Law Society model clause provided for the exclusion of such improvements by incorporating and extending the relevant wording of the Landlord and Tenant Act 1954 including 'the 21-year rule' (see Law of Property Act 1969) in most instances. Unauthorised improvements are not given this protection, however. In practice, the Valuer will have to imagine a shell in some cases devoid of tenant's improvements. The ISVA model clause on the other hand envisaged the assumption of premises fully fitted for use but then making a deduction amounting to a fair allowance for tenant's improvements. The wording of this particular clause did not appear to have been developed sufficiently.[10]

(d) *Vacant possession.* In *Langham House Developments Ltd* v *Brompton Securities Ltd* [1980] 2 EGLR 117, it was held that unless the valuation is specifically required to be carried out on the basis of vacant possession, regard can be had to the rents achieved from actual subletting. This may be disadvantageous to a landlord who would therefore normally prefer there to be an express clause requiring valuation to be on the basis of vacant possession.

(e) *Other lease terms.* Generally, the other covenants to be assumed are those which are contained in the lease and the tenant is assumed to be observing his covenants.

(f) *Date of valuation.* The date of the rent review should normally be the date of the valuation. The Courts may have to decide whether or not evidence from after the review date is admissible in an arbitration. In *Segama NV* v *Penny Le Roy Ltd* [1984] 1 EGLR 109, the Learned Judge said: 'if rent of comparable premises had been agreed on the day after the relevant date, I cannot see that such an agreement would be of no relevance whatever to what the market rent was at the relevant date itself. If the lapse of time before the agreement for comparable premises becomes greater, then ... the evidence will become progressively unreliable as evidence of rental values at the relevant date.'

(iii) Settling Disputes

If agreement cannot be reached on the current amount of rent on a rent review, the matter will be settled by an independent expert or an arbitrator. An arbitrator listens to evidence from both parties and normally decides on a figure within the range of those put forward, whereas an expert may or may not take note of evidence from the parties and arrive at his own independent figure which (occasionally) may fall outside the range of those suggested by the parties.

If an expert is to be appointed, it is essential that the lease should provide for, or the parties should agree upon, the full details of his terms of reference and the means by which the procedure should be put into effect. If such details are not available in the case of the appointment of an arbitrator he will follow the procedure in the Arbitration Act 1950. In the absence of agreement to the contrary, the lease will normally provide for an arbitrator to be appointed by the President of the Royal Institution of Chartered Surveyors. The PACT (Professional Arbitrator on Court Terms) Scheme has been devised to provide an alternative method to court litigation. It provides a scheme to allow landlords and tenants who are in agreement to decide the terms of lease outside of the courts.

Geared Ground Rents

With regard to a ground rent 'geared' to the rack rent, in the case of multi-let properties or developments it may be fairer to the head-lessee for the ground rent to be geared to the rents actually being collected rather than to an assessed rack rental value. This would allow for the possibility of voids, but on the other hand the ground landlord must be protected against an incompetent head-lessee, and the form of wording should cover this. Where the rent relates to more than the pure land there is danger in the case of 'upwards only' clauses of the rent exceeding the rents being collected by the head-lessee towards the end of the lease, when the buildings are nearing or at the end of their economic lives, and it might be wise to make some contingent arrangement for this.

Index-Linked Rents and Options to Break

As an alternative to reviewing to open market rental value, it is possible to link rent reviews to some published index such as the cost-of-living index or the construction cost index. This should protect the income from inflation, but it is an artificial concept, relying as it does on changes in values other than that of the particular property for which rent is actually being paid. This may result in the rent at any time being less or more than the open market rent, depending on how property rents, and rents relating to the relevant type of property in particular, have moved in relation to the general cost of living or cost of construction. Index-linked rents are the practice in some European countries, as is the practice of allowing tenants an option to break the lease. This combination has meant that when the cost of living has risen at a greater rate than rents, tenants in some cases took the first opportunity to break their leases leaving landlords to relet at the (lower) market rents. It is for this reason that options to break leases at rent reviews are generally resisted by landlords despite pressure from tenants from overseas. Unless landlord and tenant have got the Court's authority to exclude the relevant provision of the Landlord and Tenant Act 1954, a break could be used by the tenant in a time of deflationary rental movements to obtain a new lease at a lower market rent, thus negating an upwards only review clause.

In the case of special properties for which there may be no comparables, thus presenting valuation problems, it may be desirable to link the rent review to the level of open market rent applicable to some other form of property which it is possible to value easily.

Turnover Rents

Yet another alternative to the review to rack rent is in the case of shops, to link the rent review to the turnover. This is sometimes done to attract tenants to a new development where the level of turnover is difficult to forecast and the level of rents difficult to estimate. A formula such as a basic rent plus a percentage of turnover is frequently adopted in such cases. Turnover rents have been applied to some of the units in Hammerson's development at Brent Cross, and at Capital and Counties Eldon Square scheme in Newcastle. Also at The Ridings Centre, Wakefield. Typically such an arrangement might provide for a basic rental of, say, 80% of full rental value (but sometimes nearer to 100%) plus a percentage of gross turnover, say, 7%, or for a percentage over a certain basic figure of turnover.

The advantages of such a system to the Landlord include the fact that increases will be at annual rather than five-yearly intervals. In addition, the Landlord can often avoid losing out on rental growth in the interval between the agreement of a pre-letting and the opening of the scheme, as this growth will be a reflection of improving retail sales. A landlord is also provided with a better understanding of his tenants' businesses. Better estate management is possible. For example, weaker tenants can be spotted at an early stage. There are, however, disadvantages of such a scheme to both landlord and tenant. It is common practice to value the turnover element by reference to a higher yield than the prime yield used on the base rent and this can result in a lower capital value than that produced by the traditional rack rent basis. It can also be argued that the turnover rent system is open to abuse as the landlord is to some extent in the tenant's hands with regard to the provision of information. Also, tenants may be reluctant to provide information which they may regard as confidential, for fear of it falling into the hands of a competitor. In addition, it should be pointed out that although a weak tenant may be identified in such a scheme, he cannot necessarily be weeded out as a result of statutory protection and weak tenants may indeed receive a measure of protection with total rent payable being less than the rack rent.

References

1 Bowden, M. 'Landlord and tenant update – July 2000', *Journal of Property Investment and Finance*, Vol. 18, No. 6, 2000, pp. 641–647.
2 Nabarro Nathanson, 'Landlord and tenant update', *Journal of Property Investment and Finance*, Vol. 18, No. 4, 2000, pp. 521–527.
3 Freeman, D.J. 'Landlord and tenant issues: new developments', Website: djfreeman.co.uk, April 27 2001.
4 Baum, A. (ed) *The Property Industry*, Freeman Publishing, 2000.
5 See *supra*, note 1.
6 See *supra*, note 3.
7 See *supra*, note 3.
8 *Chartered Surveyor*, April 1980.
9 Penfield, D. 'ISVA Aim for Easier Rent Reviews', 271EG1154.
10 Freedman, D. 'ISVA Model Clauses', 272EG231.

Further Reading

'Some Aspects of Modern Leasing Considerations for Occupational Leases of Offices', *Chartered Surveyor*, July 1976.
Williams, D.W. 'Recent Trends in Rent Reviews', 271EG18; 'User Clause and Rent Reviews', 271EG1001.

The Economic and Legal Framework

Further Reading

Balchin, P.N., Kieve, J.L. and Bull, G.H. *Urban Land Economics and Public Policy*, Macmillan, 1995.
Baum, A. *Statutory Valuations*, Routledge & Kegan Paul, 1986.
Eve, Gerald & Co. *Turnover Rents for Retail Property*, 1984–85.
Fraser, W.D. *Principles of Property Investment and Pricing*, Macmillan, 1993.
Millington, A. 'Accuracy and the Role of the Valuer', 276EG260.

PART II

INVESTMENT VALUATION

Chapter Five

Principles of Valuation

A valuer may be asked to provide a valuation on a basis other than market value such as for insurance purposes. Normally his instructions are, however, to provide an estimate of market value. Opinions between valuers vary and therefore it is not necessarily to be expected that professional opinions of value will precisely equate with market value. Valuations, normally being based on market evidence, are more likely to be accurate during stable conditions. In unstable conditions there may be little market evidence or such evidence may rapidly go out of date, and in these circumstances valuers must be able to read very closely the trends of the market. The judgment in *Singer & Friedlander* v *John D Wood & Co* [1977] 2 EGLR 84 provides some interesting comments on tolerable margins of opinion.

Accuracy in valuation has received considerable attention. Amongst criticism from outside the profession came the Hager/Lord report.[1] This was submitted to the Institute of Actuaries in 1985 and purported to show inconsistencies in valuations among professional firms. A reply to the criticisms has come forward from within the profession. The reader is referred to the original documents in each case to form his own opinion on the matter.[2]

Methods of Valuation

There are five standard recognised methods of valuation and these are explained briefly below. These methods are not necessarily mutually exclusive; the comparative and investment methods always interacting for example. In valuing a hotel, both the comparative and the profits method may be relevant, and in the valuation of unusual properties generally, the valuer will have to use his experience and knowledge in deciding which method or combination of methods to use.

The comparative and the investment method are the most important to valuers, and hence the former, which may be said to underpin all the methods, warrants elaboration in a separate section of this chapter, and the latter, forming part of a central theme in this book, receives considerable attention in later chapters.

(i) The Comparative Method

The comparative method of valuation entails analysing transactions to determine the price or rent achieved and then applying the information to the property to be valued. Whether it is rental value or capital value which it is sought to determine will depend on whether the type of property is normally let or sold with vacant possession. Dwellings let on statutorily controlled rents present a potential problem to the valuer in that, although they are let to produce an income, a speculator purchaser may be more interested in the possibility of making a capital gain on obtaining vacant possession. Such properties are therefore often valued as a percentage of their vacant possession value – say 50% or whatever the particular circumstances warrant.

Ideally the comparative method should only be used when the properties being compared are similar and in the same area; where there are efficient records of frequent recent transactions; and where the market is relatively stable. In practice it may be necessary to make a valuation when one or more of these conditions is not present. For example, the market may be at a low ebb and evidence may be sparse. In this situation the valuer will have to use his knowledge and experience to interpret information which he would otherwise seek to avoid using, such as evidence of transactions from the not so recent past or from areas outside that in which the subject property lies.

It is axiomatic that the more homogeneous a class of property, the easier it is to compare properties one with another within that class. Within the commercial sector, modern offices or factories in similar areas are easier to compare than say shops, which vary greatly according to individual position.

No two properties can ever be identical, because their locations will always differ. In comparing one property with another, this and other differences must be borne in mind and taken into account.

Such differences might include the position, the plot size, the floor area, the number and arrangement of rooms, the architectural design, the age and condition, and any special features.

(ii) The Investment Method

This method is used for valuing properties which are normally held as income-producing investments. The value of such an investment is the product of the net income and the inverse of the market yield, and an example was given in Chapter 1 of the valuation of undated gilt-edged stock by this process.

Undated gilts produce a perpetual income, and the current yield is determined in the market. Freehold properties are deemed to produce a perpetual income for valuation purposes. This income may vary in the future as is the case with ordinary shares, and again the currently acceptable yield for these types of investment is determined by the market.

Where a freehold property is let at its full rental value and there is therefore no known reversionary element to be valued, and no recovery of capital to be provided for, an investment valuation is in its simplest form thus:

Net income × years' purchase = capital value

The years' purchase (YP) is the expression given to the inverse of the yield, and the net income represents the income after deduction of landlord's irrecoverable outgoings.

(iii) The Profits (or Accounts) Method

Where comparables are frequently not available, as with certain types of property such as theatres, restaurants and hotels, the valuation may have to be made purely by reference to the profits which a tenant of reasonable business acumen could make from occupation of the property. In the case of shops and offices and other 'commercial' properties, however, where comparables usually are available, a market is established and rental values can be ascertained by the more direct comparative method described above.

Where a caravan site is to be valued, for example, there are unlikely to be any recent local comparables, and the profits method may therefore be adopted. This would involve an examination of the accounts to determine typical figures. From the gross receipts would be deducted purchases and all operating and overhead costs, including an allowance for interest on tenant's capital but excluding any rent or mortgage interest payments on the property. Certain other adjustments may also need to be made. The resultant figure described as the 'divisible balance' represents the amount available for the tenant's share of remuneration and the landlord's share – rent.

This method, as with the residual and contractor's methods dealt with below, not being based on direct market evidence, is very dependent on the skill of the valuer in interpreting and manipulating the figures to produce a reliable estimate of market value.

(iv) The Residual Method

The residual method is used in valuing development sites and properties suitable for redevelopment. The method briefly involves making estimates of the cost of the project and of the value created thereby, and, after making a reasonable allowance for profit and contingency, the difference between value and cost (including a profit element) represents the value of the unimproved property. Such calculations can be carried out on a capital or a rental basis. The estimation of costs and the timing of future payments and receipts are particularly problematical.

This method is not used exclusively by developers, and may be relevant in a modified form to a prospective shop tenant for example in costing the fitting out of a 'shell unit' having regard to future value and utility. It should of course also be mentioned that the comparison method can again be brought into use in the valuation of development properties.

(v) The Contractor's Method

Properties which do not normally come onto the market, and yet are not used for profit-making enterprise, may need to be valued by the contractor's method. The types of property under consideration would include many of those owned by public authorities such as fire stations, and ambulance stations and which may need to be valued for such purposes as rating. In the context of asset valuation, the method has become known as the 'Depreciated Replacement Cost' (DRC) method.

To value by this method, an estimate must be made of the cost of replacing the site and building, and then making any necessary allowance for depreciation. The site must be valued by reference to the concept of opportunity cost. Thus the value of the site of an ambulance station in the heart of a residential area is likely to be based on the value of the land for residential development, this being the likely alternative use which would be permitted by the planning authority.

The method has the inherent disadvantage of attempting to equate cost to value, as well as certain practical difficulties involved in making the various estimates, and in particular the correct depreciation allowance. For rating purposes for example, it will be necessary to rentalise the capital figure. In this case the rate of interest to be adopted may prove problematical.[3]

Comparison

Comparison is the cornerstone of valuation. It is used not only in the valuation of property but the valuation of Stock Exchange investments, works of art, antiques, second-hand cars, and other commodities or investments where there is a relatively fluid market. Hence means of comparison in the property investment field are considered in some detail in this section.

Units of Comparison

Two properties may be so similar that if the value of one is known, it may be applied directly as the value of the other. This frequently occurs where a number of new properties have been built which for all practical purposes are the same as one another. Examples of this would include flats within a block, standard shop units on a new parade, or new factory units of similar size and design on the same estate.

In the case of commercial properties and sites for commercial property, provided the design of any buildings is standard and meets modern requirements, the chief variable for properties in the same locality is likely to be size. Thus it is usual to compare such properties according to area. Assuming a minimum standard ceiling height, cubic content of buildings may be irrelevant except that an excessive ceiling height may cost more to heat and clean or alternatively could be used for storage.

If floor areas of buildings are to be compared, it follows that the method of measurement should be consistent. Unfortunately in practice this is not always the case, and the point should be borne in mind when using information supplied by third parties, although an attempt has now been made to regularise the position with the publication of the document 'Code of Measuring Practice'.[4] Except in the valuation of industrial units, it is normal for net lettable floor space to be measured: this would exclude lift shafts, stairwells, corridors, WCs and other areas essential to the use of the building regardless of size. Areas such as store cupboards, which may be regarded as additional features, should be measured separately as in the subsequent valuation the valuer may decide that a different value per metre or square foot should be applied to such space. Industrial units are normally measured on a gross internal basis. The important maxim in valuation of 'as you analyse so shall you value' applies here as elsewhere. If information supplied is on the basis of gross internal floor area then clearly this is the way in which it must be applied to the subject of the valuation.

In the case of hi-tech buildings, a new basis of measurement is needed as offices and industrial properties are measured differently. There is no general consensus on the point as to whether these relatively new types of buildings should be measured gross or net internal. The trend seems to be to a net internal basis.

The value of a site for commercial development is dependent upon the amount and value of the floor space which can be provided according to the planning permission available. It is therefore common to compare such sites in terms of the amount of floor space which can be provided, leaving it to the valuer to judge the value of that space. Hence the value of site A may be twice as much as that of site B, which is the same size, simply because the *plot ratio* (the ratio of gross external built floor area to site area) for A is twice that for B. But, according to the circumstances of the case, there may be factors which in the valuer's judgment militate against such a simple relationship, and these would need to be taken into account.

The simple relationship between floor area and value which is common in the valuation of commercial property is less common in the valuation of residential property and residential building land. The factors which potential tenants/purchasers of dwellings usually consider important may be far more subtle. Nevertheless, the floor area of a dwelling is frequently used as a basis for rating and fair rent assessments where dwellings are of a similar type.

Other bases of comparison may be used in the case of more specialised properties such as 'per person registered' in the case of care homes, or 'per person occupancy' in the case of hotels. In making comparisons between properties in these cases, care will need to be taken in making adjustments for the quality and type of accommodation offered and addition or subtraction may need to be made relating to the number and type of communal rooms and the size and quality of proprietors' accommodation if any.

Zoning of Shops

In considering commercial property, it is generally recognised that shops are a special case. This is because different parts of the shop may be worth different amounts.

The shop frontage and the area immediately behind are used for display and attract customers into the shop, and are therefore the most valuable. Conversely, the part at the rear of a shop may be of little use as sales space, and hence reserved for storage or other ancillary uses. Accordingly, a small proportion of the overall value is usually attributed to this area.

To take account of the foregoing it would therefore not be correct to compare shops of different sizes purely by overall floor area. Regard must be had to the fact that frontage is more important than depth. Where shops are of similar depth, this may be done by comparing frontages. Where this is not the case it is common to analyse according to 'zones' of floor area.

There are no hard and fast rules about the size and number of zones to be adopted. Practice varies according to locality and circumstances. But in the absence of contradicting circumstances it is common to divide a shop into two zones of approximately 6 metres (or 20 feet) depth each and a remainder, and to assume that the front zone (zone A) is twice as valuable as zone B per square metre or foot which in turn is twice as valuable as the remainder pro rata. This is known as the 'halving back' principle.

Upper and lower floors and storage space may be valued separately according to the evidence, and an additional value may be attributed to corner shops on account of the return frontage. Having analysed by zoning, it may be decided that a pro rata deduction should be made for a particularly large shop to take account of the economies of scale in constructing, maintaining and managing such a unit. Such a 'quantum allowance' as it is termed, may also be found to be appropriate to take account of the bargaining power of the large retail multiples. It may also be noted that in view of the considerable depth of such units which is all usable retail space, the zoning principle is frequently found to be inappropriate.

The zoning process explained above is a regular and rather arbitrary affair sometimes known as 'geometric' zoning. In a particular case, different 'natural' zones may present themselves. Thus out of a row of six shops, two may be kiosks with depths of 4 metres, two may have depths of 18 metres, and two depths of 25 metres. If the rental value of one of the kiosks is known, it may be decided that this should be applied to the valuation of a 4-metre zone A on one of the larger shops. If the rental value of one of the 18-metre deep shops is known, the valuer may decide that the natural depth for a zone B for the largest shops is 14 metres (18 metres less 4 metres), and so on. It must be emphasised, however, that these variations on the conventional geometric zoning would be extremely unusual. Kiosks of course do not lend themselves to zoning being too small and disproportionately valuable according to floor area. An alternative to zoning has been proposed which involves comparison and valuation on the basis of a combination of frontage and floor area.[5]

The hypothesis that parts of a building may be worth different amounts from other parts, possibly in regular and predictable proportion to one another, is a useful analytical concept which may be extended to other classes of property. For example, in the case of old multi-storey factories, the higher the floor the lower the value, due to inaccessibility, weak floors and stairs and other factors.

The Effect of Improvements

Owners of property frequently make the mistake of assuming that expenditure on improvements can be recouped automatically through the increase in value created thereby. However, the value of improvements, like the value of any other commodity, is determined by the forces of supply and demand in a free market, and if there is no general demand for a particular improvement then it has no open market value.

This is not to say that such improvements will not have a value to the owner if he intends to retain the property for his own occupation. In such circumstances, occupiers sometimes carry out improvements, suiting their particular trade, which may have little or no market value but the cost of which they hope to recoup through increased profits during the period of their occupancy.

The investor, however, will require a return by way of increased rent which is appropriate to the type of investment which the improved property comprises. If there is latent value in the property he will achieve more than this objective, and recoup the benefit of the development value which remained latent in the site. Thus the cost of a 10% extension to an office property would exclude the cost of acquiring the site for the extension, as this is already comprised within the property investment, and normally the investor would obtain a better return than had he sought to acquire office content of similar size on the market. Such improvements should always, therefore, be valued by the conventional method of comparison.

It should be noted that the effect of an improvement on rental value will be the same regardless of tenure – a tenant will not be prepared to pay more rent simply because his landlord holds under a short lease and wishes to recoup his expenditure. Except where considerable latent value is present, therefore, it will not normally pay an investor to improve a property unless he has the freehold or a long lease or is able to recoup his capital in some other way such as through an arrangement with his landlord.

Outgoings

In order to arrive at a net income for valuation purposes it is necessary to deduct landlord's outgoings from the gross rent receivable. The landlord's liabilities in respect of outgoings may be established by reference to the lease. In the absence of agreement on these matters there may in certain instances be statutory presumptions about the respective liabilities of the parties as under the agricultural 'model clauses' (made under the Agricultural Holdings Act 1948) for example.

The landlord will where possible have arranged to avoid liability for outgoings by granting a full repairing and insuring lease or recovering them by levying a service charge. Even in these circumstances, however, it may sometimes be prudent to make some allowance or contingency for the possibility of a tenant defaulting or for the property falling vacant or part vacant, and the landlord then becoming responsible for upkeep.

The major outgoings are dealt with in the following sections.

Repairs and Maintenance

If dilapidations need to be remedied or there are other repairs of an immediate nature to be carried out an allowance should be made for this against the capital value of the property, unless comparison is being made directly with a property in a similarly dilapidated state. Normally, however, the valuer will be concerned with annual deductions from the income.

The landlord may be responsible for internal or external repairs or a mixture of both. In any event what is required is an average annual equivalent of the cost of repairs bearing in mind that repairs and maintenance items occur at varying intervals.

Having made an inspection, it is necessary to decide the standard of maintenance which is required having regard to the type of property and the life of the building. The objectives of maintenance should also be borne in mind, whether to keep the building wind- and weather-tight and structurally stable, or whether to keep it attractive as well.

Following the inspection, a maintenance programme may be planned which then may be reviewed say every three to four years. The normal intervals for redecoration are externally every three to five years, depending on the type of paint, specification, materials, exposure and so on, and internally every seven years, although circumstances may demand flexibility. Items of repair such as to roofs, gutters, woodwork and so on may be more difficult to forecast but such matters are within the compass of the surveyor, albeit possibly one who specialises in that field.

Maintenance records may provide a useful guide to the future, provided that figures are suitably updated. Other sources of information on building maintenance costs and occupational cost data include the Building Maintenance Cost Information Service sponsored by the Royal Institution of Chartered Surveyors.

Insurances

Whether or not the landlord is responsible for paying insurance premiums, he will generally have a great interest in ensuring that proper insurance cover is taken out. This particularly relates to insurance against fire and other perils, but may also apply to other insurances, especially in the case of a multi-let building. Such other insurances might include property owner's liability, employer's liability, and insurance of lifts, engineering and electrical machinery, and boilers and pressure vessels.

If the actual premiums are known and known to reflect adequate cover, then these will obviously form the basis of the outgoing under this heading. However, estimates frequently have to be made, and in the case of insurance against fire and associated perils these should normally be calculated by applying a known insurance premium rate obtained from the company to the estimated replacement cost of the building.

Two publications are of assistance in carrying out valuations for insurance purposes.[6,7] These publications carry prices per square metre or square foot for various types of properties of varying sizes, locations and ages and taking into account other variable factors. Thus the method of assessment will normally be on the basis of floor area comparisons.

In estimating the replacement cost, however, regard should be had to such factors as modern statutory requirements on rebuilding, the redevelopment period (possibly as long as two or three years) and demolition costs, the need for identical replacement of ornate features of listed buildings, making a contingency for unknowns such as substantial sub-structures or exceptional costs of an unknown nature in the case of tower blocks. This may require the services of a quantity surveyor, and specialists for any mechanical services. Run-of-the-mill insurance valuations can however easily be carried out by general practice surveyors.

Gross external area is normally used, although occasionally gross internal area applies. Again, obviously, the valuer must be consistent in the method adopted in both analysis and valuation. To convert a capital reinstatement cost to an annual outgoing will involve the application of the appropriate premium rate, usually between £1.50 and £3.00 per £1,000. If necessary, a quotation should be obtained. In addition, loss of rent should be insured against, and it is also possible now to arrange a special policy to insure against the possibility of a refusal of planning permission for the replacement building.

In the case of obsolete buildings which it would be undesirable to replace, or those which are up for sale, it may be possible to arrange a special policy under which the market value only, as opposed to the replacement cost, needs to be insured.

Services

Landlord's services might include such matters as: lighting and cleaning common parts; maintenance of lifts; heating and (occasionally) hot water provision; maintenance of any gardens; provision of staff, such as porters, maintenance of the sprinkler system to common parts and any extras, such as maintenance of a communal aerial system; together with associated management.

The lease may enable the landlord to recover some costs of management and may require him to submit accounts to the tenant. The charge may then be based on these accounts, apportioned between the tenants, or according to some other formula. In view of inflation, it is naturally becoming increasingly uncommon for the service charge to remain fixed. If tenants are to retain a satisfactory standard of services, the charge should be reviewable, and a common review period is now annual.

Rates and Taxes

General rates, water rates, and special rates (if any) are calculated by applying the rate poundage to the rateable value. They are normally the occupier's liability, in which case the rental is said to be exclusive of rates. In certain circumstances, however, the rental may be inclusive which means that the landlord is responsible for the rates. In this case the landlord should consider by reference to the lease if he can pass on a future rates increase to the tenant by adjusting the rent through an excess rates clause. If he cannot, he should make some allowance for possible future increases. Landlords will, of course, be responsible for rates on empty properties where these are being levied.

It is normally unnecessary to deduct income tax for valuation purposes because most investment income is quoted before deduction of income tax and therefore valued on a gross basis. Also, each prospective purchaser's income tax will be different, and it is not generally possible to determine the correct rate of tax to adopt. There are exceptions to this rule which are dealt with later.

Management

This includes the cost of rent collection, supervising repairs, enforcing covenants, and so on. The cost may be incurred by employing an agent or directly by the landlord. It is normally calculated by reference to a percentage of the gross rent passing (between about 0.5% and 15%) or of the service charge. The latter seems a more sensible basis in that it is more directly related to the amount of management involved. In the case of properties let on full repairing and insuring leases there are two possible approaches. One is to ignore this outgoing reflecting the small cost involved in an adjustment to the investor's required yield. The other approach is to make a specific deduction from the rental income of the small management charge incurred. This is likely to be as low as 0.5% of the rent in the case of single unit, single properties let on full repairing and insuring leases. In any event, surveyor's charges for supervision of building and maintenance works are usually recoverable.

Voids

A percentage deduction may be made for the possibility of a void (vacancy or part vacancy) occurring, or alternatively a capital deduction may be made from the capital value of the property or an allowance be made in the rate of interest adopted on capitalisation. Such a deduction is not commonly made unless there is a real and identifiable prospect of a void. It may, for example, be found from experience that 5% of a multi-let building is regularly vacant.

Guidance to Valuers

Conditions of Engagement

Guidance to both valuers and their clients is provided by the RICS Conditions of Engagement for The Valuation of Commercial and Industrial Property, which also provides the basis of the contract under which the professional services are provided. The document covers the aims and nature of a valuation, stating that the normal basis will be 'open market value' as defined therein; the advantages of employing a qualified valuer; the need for the report to be confidential to the client and his professional advisers; the scope of the valuation including investigations and assumptions and the fact that it is not a structural survey; the need for clear instructions; the need to agree a fee; and sundry matters. Similar Conditions of Engagement exist in relation to residential property.

Asset Valuation

A property investment may need to be valued, because it is changing hands, or for remortgage purposes, or because it forms part of the portfolio of an investing institution or company, the assets of which require revaluation. In the first case, the valuation can immediately be tested through the process of negotiation or competitive bidding. In the other cases, this is not so. In such circumstances the valuer will need to have regard to any statutory rules and other guidance relevant to the valuation.

As the public has an interest in these matters there is a need for statutory regulations or professional self-regulations. The Companies Act 1967, for example, requires any significant difference between the open market value of assets and the amount shown in the balance sheet to be disclosed, and hence there is a need for regular revaluation.

In 1974 the RICS set up the Assets Valuation Standards Committee, which has subsequently produced a number of Guidance Notes which have now been consolidated with provisions for updating. Under these provisions, 'open market value' is regarded as inevitably preferable to 'going concern value' as a basis for valuation, taking into account any special value of the asset to the company. The questions of 'existing use' and 'alternative use' valuations are considered, and the depreciated replacement cost method. Guidance has been provided on the principles and procedures to be adopted when valuing on the basis of current cost accounting. Further relevant RICS guidance on valuation of assets includes guidance notes on the valuation of pension fund property assets, and the valuation and sale of plant and machinery.

The Guidance Notes were originally incorporated in the *RICS Guidance Notes on the Valuation of Assets* (2nd edition, 1981). This is concerned with valuations for company accounts, financial statements and associated documents. The Guidance Notes relate to the valuation of all fixed assets, namely land and buildings and plant and machinery. They cover valuations for investment and security purposes in addition to valuations to be incorporated into company accounts and other financial statements. They also deal with valuations in connection with takeovers and mergers, the calculation of unit prices for property funds and valuations under the Insurance Companies Act.

Negative values may arise on leasehold interests where there is an income shortfall and/or onerous covenants and dilapidations. Exceptionally, a freehold property could have a negative value due to onerous obligations. Such negative figures should be reported separately. The Guidance Notes relating to the preparation of valuations are similar to those contained in the *RICS Manual of*

Valuation Guidance Notes (see below) but not identical. Similar comments apply with regard to the Conditions of Engagement. Details are given of the information to be provided in the valuation certificate. Guidance is given on the verification of information supplied to or adopted by a valuer together with frequency of valuations and ancillary matters.

When valuing in connection with accounting for depreciation it may be necessary to make a forecast of the future life of a property and the advice generally is that such forecasts should be made within certain fairly wide bands, eg less than 20 years or more than 50 years. With regard to asset valuations for incorporation in prospectuses and circulars, in the case of land being developed or held for future development, the guidance is that valuers should not allow themselves to be drawn into a situation where they include future projections as to rental income or capital values. Such projections are the responsibility of the Directors.

Mortgage Valuations

Following some court cases and debate about valuations for loan purposes, the RICS issued 'The Valuation of Property Assets for Investment and as Security for Loans' in which it was stated that 'open market value' rather than 'forced sale' would be the usual basis of valuation, and that it was for the lender to assess the risk. The RICS has now published a manual of valuation standards which covers certain valuations for sale, purchase and mortgage purposes. These notes are fairly explicit in dealing with the matters which should be considered in arriving at a valuation, and the presentation of the report.

General

In 1981 the various guidance notes were assimilated into the *RICS Manual of Valuation Standards*. The Manual was subsequently updated and extended as the *RICS Manual of Valuation Guidance Notes*. These Guidance Notes cover such matters as valuations for sale, purchase, mortgage and miscellaneous purposes, valuation, re-inspection and re-valuation of residential properties for mortgage purposes, valuation of plant and machinery, goodwill and minerals.

These Guidance Notes stress the importance of agreeing instructions (and these will normally be on the basis of the RICS Conditions of Engagement). It is noted that valuers will sometimes be expected to express opinions upon legal issues affecting valuation. In such circumstances, the valuer will need to take care to state that any interpretation of legal documents and legal assumptions made must be checked by the client with a suitably qualified lawyer, if they are to be relied upon.

Interestingly, the Guidance Notes spell out the matters which should be taken into account by a valuer in preparing a report. These are set out below together with the author's own comments thereon.

(i) *Referencing.* This relates to the physical inspection of the property and locality. Notes should be made under this heading on such matters as the characteristics of the locality including communications and facilities, the nature and brief condition of the building itself including such matters as age, description, use, accommodation, construction, installations, amenities, services, state of repair and condition. Notes should be made with regard to site stability, and importantly, dimensions and areas of the land and buildings as necessary should be taken.

(ii) *Nature of Interest.* It will obviously be necessary to ascertain the tenure with reference to restrictions, easements, rights of way, terms of leases and details of lettings and other occupations. The valuer is not normally expected to inspect Deeds although leases should be inspected where available. Information under this heading may need to be provided on the basis of assumptions or facts gleaned from the client. Solicitors will normally be required to undertake the usual requisitions on title, searches and so forth.

(iii) *Planning and Statutory Requirements.* A telephone call to the Planning Office or a personal visit may elicit certain information on town planning, highway and other relevant matters. Apparent contravention of any statutory requirements should be noted. Again, subsequent legal enquiries by solicitors, including searches may be the only satisfactory method of obtaining answers to questions relating to, for example, outstanding statutory notices.

(iv) *Other Factors.* Rating assessments and any outgoings will need to be noted. Again, this information may need to be obtained by telephone call or personal visit to the rating office. Under this heading any plant and machinery which would normally form an integral part of the building should be noted down for inclusion in the valuation. Any non-standard methods of construction or information regarding the absence or otherwise of deleterious or hazardous materials or techniques should be considered. Information regarding the latter may not be readily available and likely assumptions may commonly be made and stated. Consideration should be given to allowances for disrepair, any development potential, and any possible breakup value.

(v) *Marketing Analysis.* Details should be noted of comparable market transactions for either existing use or alternative uses, together possibly with market conditions and trends.

(vi) *The Valuation Report.* The Valuation Report will normally include a summary of the matters referred to in paragraphs (i) to (iv) above, together with reference to the purpose, basis and date of the valuation, if with vacant possession or otherwise, together with reference to any special instructions, unusual assumptions or omissions. Limitations of responsibility will be stated with regard to the examination of the structure, the restriction of use of the report, and the assumptions of fact and of law adopted. In addition, the verification and sources of information will need to be noted, and finally and most importantly, (not to be forgotten) the opinion of value in figures and words.

Some of the above matters are amplified in the Guidance Notes. For example, the physical condition of the property is divided into four basic categories ranging from failure to redecorate, to the presence of a basic structural defect in the building. It is always necessary to make clear that the inspection and report do not purport to be a structural survey. With regard to legal matters such as the nature of the interest, town planning and other regulatory matters, it is important that if the valuer cannot check, he or she should state in the report the matters which it is considered might affect the valuation and, if appropriate, suggest that the solicitors refer back to the valuer if searches reveal matters which might affect value.

With regard to the valuation of residential properties for mortgage purposes, the Guidance Notes include such matters as disclaimer clauses in relation to reports being made available to third parties, referencing, the exclusion of price-included furnishings and removable fittings, the limitations of inspection and other ancillary matters. It is perhaps obvious but it needs to be stated that one of the main objects of the inspection is to determine precisely the exact subject matter of the valuation. Reference is made in the notes to local authority system built houses, procedure for unbuilt or partially built new dwellings, insurance valuations, and allied matters.

There has been some debate recently over the role of the mortgage valuation. It is generally accepted by the RICS guidance notes for valuers that the valuer should not make a recommendation as to the amount or the percentage of mortgage advance or as to the length of the mortgage term. The mortgage valuation has been the subject of debate in two areas. Firstly, in new house valuation where new house premiums may be taken into account. The premium relates to the fact that, as soon as the property is sold second hand, there is likely to be a discount. A solution has been suggested that the valuations be carried out on the basis of a new house with the premium, provided that it is stated that on immediate resale the value will be reduced by a certain amount.

The second debate on mortgage valuation relates to whether a warning should be given to the lender when valuing in a falling market. This would be especially important when valuing a property in the process of construction when only a small amount of building work had been carried out.

Improvements in Valuation Reports

Beyond the Guidance Notes, one criticism is the general failure of valuation reports to provide reasons for recommendations or to state the assumptions underlying valuations. This is liable to detract from the value of the report to the client who needs to make a decision on the basis of the report. It has been suggested that typical important matters which should be included (and in the future the inclusion of these matters may become the norm) are as follows:

(a) the rental growth anticipated by the Valuer and the speed of such growth;
(b) the opportunity cost of capital (or the cost of borrowing) considered appropriate and used in the valuation;
(c) allowances made for future repairs, rental voids, management expenses, and other similar outgoings; and
(d) the period of years over which future income flow has been anticipated, and whether any consideration has been made for the possible need for major refurbishment or even complete redevelopment at some future date.[8]

Difficulties may arise where the value of a portfolio as a whole exceeds the sum of the values of the constituent parts and valuers have been known to add 10% to the sum of the parts to arrive at the value of the whole. Guidance notes issued by the Assets Valuation Standards Committee of the RICS deal with this matter. They allow for special assumptions and purchasers who have a particular interest and this may be applied to valuations in the context of takeovers. These guidelines provide for a two-stage approach to the valuation, the first being the normal open market value approach, and the second drawing attention to the potential which may arise from a special reasonable assumption, such as obtaining planning permission in the foreseeable future.

Criticisms and court cases reflecting the alleged negligence of professional valuers has led to some reconsideration of the advice given to purchasers. The problem may, of course, relate to a decline in the market whereby mistakes related to the calculation of market value at the time of transaction are not upheld by subsequent evidence. The Mallinson Report commissioned by the RICS and properly called the President's Working Party on Commercial Property Valuations reported in March 1994. The Chairman suggested that there were four key areas which are described as needs or requirements of the valuer undertaking these commercial property evaluations. These so-called needs are:

(i)   Valuers need to be able to demonstrate to clients that, although there are many valuers who would make different judgements, all work is within a common body of knowledge, application and expression. Differences will therefore be as narrow as possible, and where they occur they will be reasonable and explicable, not perverse or chaotic.

(ii) Valuers need to demonstrate that the profession is regulated, not in a purely bureaucratic sense, but that valuers perform their task in an organised manner, not in a maverick or inspirational way, that they take care to educate themselves, and that they are subject to discipline.

(iii) Valuers need to be able to express more clearly what they do and what they do not do. It is not possible to 'make clients understand', nor is it tenable to urge that 'clients should be educated'. Care and precision in explanation will do much to achieve both ends.

(iv) Valuers need to improve the technical element of their skill, updating and extending their mathematical models, their access to and use of data, and their expression of the relativities of their judgement. They should not assume their task to be limited to the production, as if from a hat, of a final figure.

The main proposals of the Mallinson Report are that there be a greater dialogue between valuers and their clients leading to clearer instructions, a summary of which would accompany the valuation figure. A second proposal is the right for valuers to ensure that shareholders receive the statement explaining property valuations in company accounts. In addition, the report proposed closer liaison between valuers and auditors, with direct access to audit committees. In addition, the report proposes that there be increased investigatory powers for the RICS in cases of public concern or at the client's request. The report recommends that valuations need to contain more comment on valuation risk factors, price trends and economic factors. Refined discounted cashflow techniques and research on concepts of 'worth' need to be developed. Finally, the report also suggests that there be a wider availability of data which is necessary for valuations and that the definition of open market value should be retained but its title changed to 'defined value' or 'defined notional price'.[9]

It was hoped that these proposals would go some way towards dealing with the disquiet which has arisen over a number of cases. It is to be noted that this is not just a problem of valuation in the UK, as can be noted from the collapse of the Jurgen Schneider Property Group in Germany and which is likely to have a lasting effect on the German property market because of the size of the collapse. Some of the blame relating to this collapse has been put on the poorly trained and organised German valuers whose valuations methods and education were suggested to be below those of the international standard. A German society of valuation surveyors has been formed to correct this.[10]

The 'Red Book'

The Mallinson Committee report[11] advised that the previous 'Red Book' (guidelines used for valuing assets) and the 'White Book' (guidelines used for mortgage valuation and other specialist areas) should be merged. In September 1995, the Royal Institution of Chartered Surveyors' *Appraisal and Valuation Manual* was published.[12] This manual provides the minimum required standards expected of professionals in practice and is mandatory from January 1996 onwards for members of the appropriate valuation institutions (the RICS and the Institute of Revenue Rating). The new 'Red Book' is in two parts: the Practice Statements and the Guidance Notes. The Practice Statements apply to all types of valuation and are mandatory along with the appendices. The Guidance Notes are not mandatory but provide information on good practice and supercede the previous Guidance Notes. The 'Red Book' contains a number of definitions, including:

Appraisal: the written provision of a valuation, combined with professional opinion or advice on the suitability of the subject property for a defined purpose.

Estimation of worth: the provision of a written estimate of the net monetary worth of the subject property to the client.

Valuation: the provision of a written opinion as to the price or value of the subject property on any given basis. It is specifically not a forecast, which in turn is defined as the prediction of the likely value on a stated basis at a future specified date.

These valuation bases are agreed with the client prior to the valuation and should be appropriate to the client's needs but cannot override statutory definitions. The calculation of worth is distinguished from calculations for market value or open market value. Open market value starts from the assumption that parties to the transaction acted knowledgeably, prudently and without compulsion. Market value appears the same as open market value but appears as the definition used by the International Valuation Standing Committee.[13] The 'Red Book' defined open market value as:

> An opinion of the best practice at which the sale of an interest in property would have been completed unconditionally for cash consideration on the date of valuation, assuming:
> (a) a willing seller;
> (b) that, prior to the date of valuation, there had been a reasonable period (having regard to the nature of the property and the state of the market) for the proper marketing of the interest, for the agreement of the price and terms and for the completion of the sale;
> (c) that the state of the market, level of values and other circumstances were, on any earlier assumed date of exchange of contracts, the same as on the date of valuation;
> (d) that no account is taken of any additional bid by a prospective purchaser with a special interest; and
> (e) that both parties to the transaction had acted knowledgeably, prudently and without compulsion.[14]

The 'Red Book', as previously mentioned, is divided into practice statements and guidance notes. Practice Statement 1 covers appraisal and valuations for all purposes including Home Buyers Reports and mortgage valuations. Practice Statement 2 relates to the requirement to understand the needs of the client and sets down the basic criteria that the valuer would need to identify. The following criteria are the basis of valuation: the subject property; the purpose of the valuation; any assumptions to be made; and the date of the valuation. In addition, it should be clear, firstly, whether information will be required from the client for the valuation to be made, secondly, what the currency of the report is and thirdly, the limitations to third-party use and restrictions on publication. Practice notes 5–7 go on to examine special circumstances related to the report: the database of comparables, the record of analysis and, finally, the minimum requirements of the reports (for instance the need to check whether the valuation report being provided will be included in the company accounts). Statements 8–22 list special requirements for reports if these conflict with general guidance given.

There is a continuing debate about estimated realisation price (ERP) and whether it will resolve or compound problems of credibility which gave rise to the need for the Mallinson report in the first place. Estimated realisation price requires the valuer to consider what changes are likely to occur in the market for the property during the marketing period; this includes external factors such as quality of the location, etc. It is the open market value but with completion assumed after the date of valuation and where the valuer is required to specify an appropriate marketing period. One view of this innovation is that there is now a need for the valuer to look forward into the future in providing valuation advice and that this forecasting has been imposed on the profession by lending institutions. This view suggests that the result of this could be more, rather than fewer, claims for negligence against valuers. The change for the profession in this relates to the way the old 'Red Book' referred to the need for relevant experience in carrying out professional practice, while the concentration in the new 'Red Book' is on the valuer's knowledge, understanding and skills.[15] The new definition of ERP was needed following pressure from secured lenders who believed that the existing definition of open market value required the marketing period to be retrospective, ending at the date of valuation and expecting the valuer to look backwards. The valuer in using the traditional 'open market value' was therefore telling the lender only what in effect, he already knew and did not supply what he wanted to know, which was an assessment of the security provided by the property in the future.

References

1 Hager, D. and Lord, D. 'The Property Market, Property Valuations and Property Performance Measurement', *Estates Gazette*, January 26 1985 and February 2 1985.
2 Reed, I. 'A Response to Hager/Lord', 274EG19.
3 Leach, W.A. 'Contractors Method and Interest Rates', 273EG567.
4 RICS, *Code of Measuring Practice*.
5 Smith, K.R. 'A Consideration of the Zoning Principle', 270EG388.
6 RICS, *Reinstatement Assessments for Insurance Purposes*.
7 *The British Insurance Association, Annual Guide to House Rebuilding Costs for Insurance Valuation*, Building Cost Information Service, RICS.
8 Millington, A. 'Accuracy and the Role of the Valuer', 276EG260.
9 *Property Week*, April 21 1994, p.4.
10 *Property Week*, April 21 1994, p.8.
11 Royal Institution of Chartered Surveyors, *President's Working Party on Commercial Property Valuations (Mallinson Report)*, RICS, London, March 1994.
12 Royal Institution of Chartered Surveyors, *RICS Appraisal and Valuation Manual*, RICS, London, 1995.
13 'The new Red Book', *Estates Gazette*, January 6 1996, pp. 96–7.

14 See *supra*, note 12.
15 See *supra*, note 15.

Further Reading

Chapman, J. 'Pension funds and insurance companies', 265EG106.
Stapleton, T. 'Appraisal of leisure property', EG Issue 8904.

Chapter Six

The Mathematics of Valuation and Finance

Valuation Tables

For valuers, mathematics is not an end in itself, but may be part of a means to an end. Certain formulae are available for valuers to use in different situations. These formulae have been worked out for a wide range of data in a comprehensive set of valuation tables (*Parry's Valuation and Investment Tables*).[1] In the early editions of *Parry's* it was necessary to refer to different sets of tables for different assumptions. *Parry's* for a long period has contained tables where the income is receivable quarterly in advance as an alternative to where it is received annually in arrears. In both cases, interest is converted (or credited) annually. Previously, the quarterly in advance information was only available in *Rose's Tables*.[2] As an alternative to this, *Bowcock's Tables*[3] were available and contained the assumption that the income was receivable quarterly in advance and interest converted half-yearly. This is not the assumption used in this book. *Bowcock's Tables* and *Rose's Tables* are now no longer available. Alternatively and particularly where the data is beyond the scope of any of the published tables, the valuer can use a computer or calculator to compute the required figures.

The formulae upon which the various tables are based are now considered. Different notations are in use in the financial and valuation worlds, and in order to make easy comparisons a common notation has generally been adopted in this section – this being the traditional valuation notation.

Amount of £1

Formulae:
Interest converted annually $(1 + i)^n$
Interest converted at less than annual intervals

$$\left(1 + \frac{i}{m}\right)^{mn}$$

i = nominal rate of interest per annum expressed as a decimal
n = number of years
m = number of times interest is converted in a year

This table is the basic compound interest table showing the amount to which £1 invested now will accumulate in a given number of years at a given rate of interest.

Thus £1 invested now for 5 years at 10% nominal pa accumulates to $(1 + 0.1)^5 = £1.6105$, where interest is converted annually or $\left(1 + \frac{0.1}{2}\right)^{2 \times 5} = £1.6289$, where interest is converted half-yearly.

Most interest rates quoted are annual rates, but these are only true rates of interest if interest is indeed converted annually. If interest is converted at less than annual intervals then the true rate is higher and the quoted rate becomes only a nominal rate. Thus £1,000 invested now will accumulate to £1,100 after one year if 10% is converted annually, but will accumulate as follows if the nominally quoted 10% pa rate of interest is converted half-yearly:

Amount invested	£1,000
First half-year's interest 5% of £1,000	50
Principal carried forward	£1,050
Second half-year's interest 5% of £1,050	52.50
	£1,102.50

The interest earned is £1,102.50 – £1,000 = £102.50, and the effective rate of interest is:

$$\frac{102.5}{1,000} \times 100 = \underline{10.25\%}$$

The formula for converting a nominal rate of interest to an effective rate of interest is:

$$\left(1 + \frac{i}{m}\right)^m - 1$$

Therefore the true rate of interest in the above example could have been calculated thus:

$$\left(1 + \frac{0.1}{2}\right)^2 - 1 = 0.1025 \text{ or } \underline{10.25\%}$$

Present Value of £1 (PV of £1)

This shows the amount which if invested now will accumulate to £1 in a given number of years. The formulae are the reciprocals of the respective formulae for the Amount of £1, thus:

$$\frac{1}{(1 + i)^n} \quad \text{or} \quad \frac{1}{\left(1 + \dfrac{i}{m}\right)^{mn}}$$

Example 6.1

How much will need to be invested now to accumulate to £1,000 in 4 years' time assuming interest at 12% per annum nominal credited half-yearly.

$$\text{PV £1} = \frac{1}{\left(1 + \dfrac{0.12}{2}\right)^8} = 0.627$$

$$\times \text{ £1,000} = \underline{£627}$$

Amount of £1 Per Annum

This shows the amount which will accumulate if £1 is invested each year for a given number of years. The traditional approach is to assume £1 to be invested at the end of each year and the formula is:

$$\frac{(1 + i)^n - 1}{i}$$

An alternative assumption is £0.25 to be invested quarterly in advance using the formula:

$$\frac{(1 + r)^n - 1}{4[1 - (1 + r)^{-1/4}]}$$

where r is the effective annual rate of interest.

Annual Sinking Fund

This shows the amount which must be invested each year to accumulate to £1 in a given number of years. The formulae are the reciprocals of those for the Amount of £1 per annum.

Annuity £1 will Purchase

This shows the annual return over a given number of years on an investment of £1 where the return comprises equal annual instalments, each consisting in part of interest on original capital and in part of an amount which if invested in an annual sinking fund would recoup the original capital outlay. This is known as an annuity type investment for which the traditional formulae are $(i + s)$ where s is the annual sinking fund instalment, or $\dfrac{i}{(1 - PV)}$

where PV is the Present Value of £1.

It will be noted that part of the annual return is for investment in a sinking fund. If it is to be assumed that the rate of interest payable on the sinking fund (known as the *accumulative rate*) is the same as that payable on the invested capital (known as the *remunerative rate*), this is known as the *single rate* principle. The *dual rate* principle, on the other hand, is based on the assumption that the remunerative and accumulative rates are different.

Years' Purchase (YP)

This shows the amount which must be invested now to produce a return of £1 per annum over a given number of years, the return consisting in part of interest on original capital and in part of an amount which if invested in an annual sinking fund would recoup the original capital outlay.

The formulae are the reciprocals of those for the Annuity £1 will purchase, and the single rate and dual rate principles apply.

Where the investment is of a perpetual nature there is no need for a sinking fund, or in terms of mathematics the sinking fund instalment becomes infinitely small, and the formula is reduced to: $\dfrac{1}{i}$.

An alternative way of constructing the YP single rate (assuming annually in arrear income) is to regard each unit of income separately and then to multiply it by the PV £1 for the period which will elapse before it is received. The sum of the PV's £1 becomes the YP single rate for the appropriate number of years. Hence the alternative name of this YP, the Present Value of £1 per annum. Mathematically this is a geometric progression which may be reduced to the formula: $\dfrac{(1 - PV)}{i}$.

With regard to the quarterly in advance tables, the YP may also be constructed by the addition of the successive PVs, provided it is realised that the first quarter of the income is received immediately. The subsequent quarters would then need each to be multiplied by the appropriate PV for the quarter or number of quarters in question.[4]

The tables of YP and PV £1 are those most commonly used by valuers because valuers are generally required to estimate the value today of income or capital receivable in the future. These tables are known as discounting tables and the rate of interest adopted is commonly called the discount rate, although where the YP is used it is also known as the capitalisation rate. This is because the PV £1 tables are used to discount future capital sums to a present value. The YP is used to capitalise an income stream into the future to a present capital sum.

Deferred Incomes

Valuers are often required to capitalise an income flow which, instead of commencing immediately, is deferred for a number of years. The usual way of dealing with this is to multiply the PV £1 for the period of deferment by the YP for the period of the income flow.

Example 6.2(a)

Value the right to receive a fixed income of £1,000 per annum net annually in arrears for 10 years deferred 5 years on the single rate basis assuming a discount rate of 15%.

Answer

Net income		£1,000 pa
YP 10 yrs @ 15%	5.0188	
× PV £1 5 yrs @ 15%	0.49718	2.4952
Capital value (to nearest pound)		£2,495

Because the YP single rate is the sum of the PVs for the period in question, it follows that by deducting the YP for the period of deferment from the YP for the total of the period of deferment plus the period of the income flow, one is left with effectively a deferred YP for the period of the income flow. Thus the deferred YP in the above example could have been calculated thus:

YP 15 yrs (5 yrs plus 10 yrs)	@ 15%	5.8474
Less: YP 5 yrs	@ 15%	3.3522
Deferred YP		2.4952

Where dual rate tables are used this second method is not appropriate as the dual rate YP does not represent the sum of the PVs, and the only correct method is that of multiplying the PV by the YP dual rate.

Example 6.2(b)

Repeat the above calculation but on a dual rate basis, assuming a sinking fund accumulating at 4% per annum.

Net income		£1,000	pa
YP 10 years @ 15% & 4%	4.2865		
× PV £15 years @ 15%	0.49718		2.1312
Capital Value (to nearest pound)			£2,131

Published tables are available to value a perpetual income receivable after an initial period of deferment. The table is referred to as the *years purchase of a reversion to a perpetuity*, and the formulae are:

$$\frac{1}{i} \times PV \ (\textit{Parry's annually in arrear}) \text{ and}$$

$$\frac{(1 + r)^{-n}}{4[1 - (1 + r^{-\frac{1}{4}})]} \quad (\textit{Bowcock's quarterly in advance})$$

The Practical Effect of the Different Assumptions

Bowcock's Tables are produced on the assumption that when one refers to a nominal rate of return of say 8%, one is almost invariably talking about an effective rate of return slightly higher than this. This is because most investments have less than annual conversions of interest, and because Bowcock considers that most investment interest is converted on a half-yearly basis. This may be so, although evidence shows a variety of methods of conversion.[5,6] Hence *Parry's* uses the annual conversion of interest assumption.

If one is prepared to accept annual conversions of interest, then the traditional *Parry's* tables can be used to make calculations on the basis of income receivable at other than annual intervals in arrears. For example, to convert *Parry's* YP single rate to annually in advance, it is only necessary to add one to the figure given in the table to allow for the immediate receipt of £1. By way of further example, if the column headed 'year' can be read as a column headed 'Periods' then a YP based on income received at other than annual intervals can be obtained. For example, it may be required to capitalise an income of £10,000 per annum receivable quarterly in arrears over two years at 8% per annum. The procedure would be to divide both the income and the rate percent by four to produce £2,500 and 2% respectively and then use the YP for eight periods of 2% multiplied by an income of £2,500. The only problem here is that if the income is receivable at less than annual intervals then to achieve a return of 8% per annum, slightly less than 2% per quarter can be accepted as the interest received in the early quarters can be re-invested.[5]

In this connection it may be necessary to be more precise about the meaning of the term 'Yield'. It is the *effective annual yield* on an investment which is important in this context and this has been defined as follows:[7]

'The single sum of money income (%), which if received in one sum at the *end* of the year would be equivalent to the accumulation of all the sums actually received *during* the year, allowing for the interest which these latter sums could earn if suitably invested between their receipt and the end of the year.'

In the case of perpetual incomes if analyses of comparables are carried out to determine YP and YPs are used as the basis of comparison, then the different assumptions will not affect the valuation.

Example 6.3

Value the freehold interest in a rack rented office investment producing a net income of £50,000 per annum payable quarterly in advance. A similar investment producing £60,000 per annum has just sold for £1,000,000.

Stage 1: analyse comparable for YP

$$\frac{1,000,000}{60,000} = 16.6$$

Stage 2: valuation (assuming investments directly similar)

Net income	£50,000	pa
YP	16.6	
	£833,333	

Such a valuation can be carried out without reference to valuation tables. Examples of situations where the effects of the differing assumptions do come into play, however, are as follows:

(i) Where the investor requires to know the effective annual yield on the investment.
(ii) Where the properties being compared produce different timing of income flows.
(iii) In the valuation of leasehold and reversionary investments.

Accuracy in Valuations

Although valuation is not an exact science, it is still the job of the valuer to make the most realistic assumptions in a given situation and then to carry out the appropriate calculations. This may not always be easy. For example, rents covenanted to be paid quarterly in advance may in practice be paid somewhat in arrears by the tenants. Valuers should not rigidly use one particular set of assumptions but should think about the circumstances of the particular valuation.

One matter which has received little attention until recent times is the *apportionment* procedure adopted by solicitors on completion of a transaction. Such a procedure appears to originate from the Apportionment Act 1870. Although this does not make apportionment an essential legal requirement, the procedure is in fact contained in both the Law Society's and National Conditions of Sale. For example, if rent is receivable annually in arrears and completion takes place six months prior to the rent day, then half of that year's rent will be deemed to be due to the vendor and therefore payable on completion by the purchaser who will, in due course, be receiving that payment from the tenant as part of the full year's rent at the end of the year. If it were not for this apportionment procedure the use of conventional YPs would produce incorrect results. The value of the investment would be dramatically different just before and just after the rent day. The effect is similar to that which determines the market price for gilt-edged stock just before and just after the stock is declared 'ex dividend'.

While the apportionment procedure works reasonably well with regard to freeholds, it does not produce reasonable results when applied to leaseholds and particularly short leaseholds. One problem relates to the fact that the date of completion will not be known at the date of valuation or agreement although an 'effective date of completion' can be agreed. However, it may occur that the case is not remitted back to the valuers for further consideration if there is a delay in completion. Such a delay in completion could have a dramatic effect on the yield to the purchaser under the present apportionment arrangements.

The problem with regard to leaseholds could be resolved if the apportionment only applied to the remunerative part of the income. Alternatively, the conditions of sale would need to be altered to provide for no apportionment and the effects would need to be reflected in the valuation (to be finally adjusted immediately prior to exchange of contracts).

Other associated problems are the question of whether or not the value is the amount agreed between the valuers or the amount which appears on the contract which will reflect apportionments. If the valuation is not in the context of a sale as, for example, an asset valuation, there will be no apportionments to be made by the solicitors on completion and therefore should the valuation reflect any apportionment which would be made on a sale? If an asset is to be retained then the owner of the investment is entitled to all future rents in full. The question posed here is similar in principle to that with regard to acquisition and disposal costs which are often taken into account in valuations for sale but would not strictly be incurred if the asset being valued remains unsold. These questions do not appear to have been fully resolved at the time of writing.

Finally, under this heading it should be noted that *Parry's* annually in arrears tables are the most familiar to valuers. They have been adopted in the examples used in the remainder of this book (except where indicated to the contrary). The differing assumptions between the tables will usually be immaterial to the principle being explained.

Discounted Cash Flow

General Principles

The technique of discounted cash flow (DCF) has been developed primarily by economists and accountants as a tool in the decision-making process. It is used to assess the profitability of investment projects given certain criteria. It may be used to calculate whether or not a particular project meets such criteria as laid down by management, or to compare projects one with another to ascertain which is the most profitable. The investment method of valuation is a simple form of DCF. However, considerable thought has been given in recent years to the possible need for a more comprehensive mathematical model, one aspect of which would be a true DCF evaluation.

To make a DCF calculation, all future costs and receipts have to be estimated and tabulated. In the case of a property valuation, the cost will normally be the original capital outlay, and the receipts will be the income generated thereby. More sophisticated appraisals may be made, however, by introducing other costs such as taxes and outgoings and by estimating the effect of future rent reviews. The timing of such future costs and revenues would then be reflected in the resultant DCF calculation. There are two major methods of making DCF calculations – the net present value (NPV) method and the internal rate of return (IRR) method – and these are considered in subsequent sections of this chapter.

According to some writers there is no need to take inflation into account in a DCF appraisal because inflation will affect all projects equally, but this is patently untrue as in the field of property investment, for example, where the frequency of rent reviews will dictate the extent to which the investment is proofed against inflation. Indeed, one of the prime reasons for introducing DCF to property valuation is so that inflation *can* be taken in account. Much of this book is concerned with this very problem.

Net Present Value (NPV)

The NPV of a project is expressed as a sum of money representing
the (discounted) present value of the flow of all income, less the
(discounted) present value of all outgoings, including capital
outlay, obtained from a project over the whole of its life. This may
be represented by the formula:

$$NPV = \sum_{i=0}^{n} \frac{a_i}{(1+r)^i}$$

where a_i is the cash flow in year i, r is the discount rate, and n is the
number of years of the project.

Example 6.4

Calculate the NPV of a project, the purchase price of which is
£8,800, and which generates the following cash flows, using a
discount rate of 10%.

		Year 1	£2,000
		Year 2	£4,000
		Year 3	£4,400
		Year 4	£2,200

Year	Cash Flow	PV £1 @ 10%	Present Value
1	£2,000	0.909	£1,818
2	£4,000	0.826	£3,304
3	£4,400	0.751	£3,304
4	£2,200	0.683	£1,503
			£9,929
		Less outlay	£8,800
		NPV	+ £1,129

The following points should be noted:

(i) The *cash flows* represent the best estimates thereof. These may
be presented on either a net or gross of tax basis, but if tax is
taken into account it will normally represent an outgoing in a
subsequent year to that in which the income is earned.

(ii) The *discount rate*, sometimes known as the *target rate* or *criterion
rate* may represent the rate of interest to be paid on capital
borrowed for the project. If internal funds are used to finance
the project, the discount rate may represent that rate of interest
which could normally be earned by the investor's business
activities (the personal time preference rate), or the rate of

interest which the funds could earn on external investment opportunities such as lending money (the external opportunity cost of capital). In any event, it is the marginal cost of capital which is relevant and thus must be measured on the same basis of tax liability and inflation-proof quality as are the returns and costs in the subject project. In investment appraisal, the discount rate is sometimes taken as the rate on undated government stock, or dated to coincide with the life of the project under consideration. There is no reason why alternative fixed interest securities such as debentures should not be used as a measure of comparison. The yield on equities, however, is not normally considered to be relevant as this is merely an initial yield based on an assumption of sharing in future profits, and a DCF analysis conducted on this basis would have to reflect the paying of dividend out of future cash flows.

(iii) If the NPV is positive, as in this example, the investment is worthwhile. If it is negative, this means that the criterion rate has not been achieved and the investment will be rejected. If a number of mutually exclusive projects are being compared, the one with the highest NPV may be chosen, provided that the capital outlay on each is similar. If the capital outlay on each is dissimilar, the *benefit/cost ratio* may be calculated, and this is obtained by dividing the discounted present value of the total benefits to be obtained from a project by the discounted present value of its total cost. The project with the highest benefit/cost ratio would then normally be chosen.

A variation on the NPV method where annual receipts are constant is the *Equivalent Annual Value (AEV) method*. This entails calculating the *annual equivalent* of the capital sum invested by dividing it by the years' purchase for the life of the project at the criterion rate of interest. This annual equivalent is then deducted from the annual revenue, and a positive answer indicates that the project is viable.

Internal Rate of Return (IRR)

The IRR or DCF rate of return, as it is sometimes called, is the rate by which future net receipts must be discounted so that their discounted value will exactly equal the initial cost of the project – in other words, when the NPV is zero. It therefore measures the true rate of return on the capital invested. This rate may be ascertained by setting the NPV formula equal to zero and solving for r. For this it is necessary to use an iterative technique, which is done here by discounting the annual receipts at different trial rates until that rate is found which most nearly makes the NPV equal to zero. Use of a computer enables this to be worked out quickly and accurately. However, the experienced appraiser will soon learn to judge the approximate range of rates required, and in the following example, trial rates of 15% and 16% are adopted and found to produce the required range.

Example 6.5

Using the cash flows from Example 6.4, calculate the IRR.

Year	Cash Flow	PV £1 @ 15%	Present Value	PV £1 @ 16%	Present Value
1	£2,000	0.870	£1,740	0.862	£1,724
2	£4,000	0.756	£3,024	0.743	£2,972
3	£4,400	0.658	£2,896	0.641	£2,820
4	£2,200	0.572	£1,258	0.552	£1,214
			£8,918		£8,730
Less outlay			£8,880		£8,800
NPV			+£118		−£70

At 15% a positive NPV is produced and at 16% a negative one, whereas the IRR is that rate which produces a NPV of zero. Therefore the IRR lies in the range of 15% to 16%. If NPVs are plotted on a graph against discount rates, the result is a curved line from which may be read intermediate points to determine the exact IRR. An alternative slightly inaccurate short-cut is to assume a straight-line relationship in which a change in discount rate produces an exactly proportional change in NPV. This is known as *linear interpolation*, and the IRR may be derived by this method using the following formula:

$$R_1 + \left[(R_2 - R_1) \times \frac{NPV_{R1}}{NPV_{R1} + NPV_{R1}} \right]$$

where R_1 is the lower rate and R_2 is the higher rate, and the signs (+ or −) of the NPV are ignored. Thus in the example, the correct rate is:

$$15 + \left[1 \times \frac{118}{188} \right] = 15.63\%$$

As stated, this is an approximate method and if the gap between the two interest rates is too large, the degree of approximation may be unacceptable.

If the IRR exceeds the investors opportunity cost of capital, then the investment is normally considered worthwhile.

Where the future receipts are constant for a number of years, the IRR may be found by reference to the table of years' purchase.

Example 6.6

A capital outlay of £15,000 results in an income of £4,000 per annum over 5 years. Calculate the IRR.

$$YP = \frac{15,000}{4,000} = 3.75$$

By reference to the body of the table of YP single rate for five years, it may be found that a YP of 3.75 corresponds to a rate of interest between 10% and 11%, or approximately 10.5%.

Alternatively and far more laboriously, the IRR could be found by DCF adopting trial rates of interest until the following result is obtained.

Year	Cash Flow	PV £1 @ 10–5%	Present Value
1	£4,000	0.905	£3,620
2	£4,000	0.819	£3,276
3	£4,000	0.741	£2,964
4	£4,000	0.671	£2,684
5	£4,000	0.607	£2,428
			£14,972
		Less outlay	£15,000
		NPV	– £28

This NPV is close enough to zero to produce an IRR of the order of accuracy normally required.

The above example merely illustrates that the YP single rate consists of the sum of the PVs of £1 over the life of the project, and that DCF is not required to analyse or value a simple investment consisting of a capital outlay followed by a series of regular and equal receipts.

Some Difficulties Associated with DCF

In comparing two or more projects, analysis by the NPV method and the IRR method may sometimes produce conflicting results due to the particular pattern of cash flows and interest rates involved. Where the projects are of different sizes then the conflict may be resolved by means of the benefit/cost ratio referred to earlier, or by means of *incremental yield analysis* which entails calculating the yield which the larger project produces by reference only to the additional increment of capital and the additional increments of cash flows.

Where a number of small positive cash flows are followed by a major negative flow (as may arise in practice through capital outlay on replacements, compensation payments, etc), if the cumulative total of present values changes its sign (+ or −) during the life of the project, more than one IRR may be found, or alternatively no IRR may be found. This type of investment is known as a non-conventional investment as against a conventional investment which involves a capital outlay followed by a series of receipts.

Solutions to the problem may be found, for example, by reverting to the NPV method or by using a dual-rate DCF technique involving the use of two rates of interest, one so long as the cumulative total of cash flows is negative, and another when at any time it becomes positive. These aspects of this particular problem are beyond the scope of this book, but it is as well for the reader to know that they exist. Incidentally, the dual-rate technique referred to here should not be confused with the dual rate principle as applied to years' purchase.

In the field of property these problems do not usually arise, partly because most property investments are conventional investments, and partly because the IRR and NPV methods are used for different purposes, the former for analysis and the latter (albeit in a modified form) for valuation. It is therefore probably inappropriate in this context to discuss the relative advantages and disadvantages of the two methods.

Mathematicians or Valuers?

There is an ongoing debate between traditional valuers and protagonists of explicit mathematical models. It is important to remember that the skill of a valuer rests largely in his experience and personal qualities (albeit underpinned by satisfactory mathematical models). A balanced view is needed between the necessary rigorous and conscientious procedure in the whole valuation process (including inspection, note taking, compilation of comparables etc) and the need for research and understanding of explicit mathematical models.

DCF Approaches to Valuation versus Traditional Growth Implicit Valuations

The argument of using DCF approaches against the traditional Years' Purchase approach is extensive. Problems arise because the price paid in the market may not reflect the present worth of the future cash flow and these problems relate to an earlier discussion where it was suggested that appraisal needs to distinguish between the valuation of a purchase price and the analysis of the worth of an investment. A DCF approach appears to be the only realistic approach to dealing with over-rented property and this is discussed later in the book. In the present market, the use of traditional techniques may no longer be defended. The traditional methods of the hardcore approach and the term and reversion are examined later in Chapter 9, but these may not be able to cope with issues such as rent-free periods, reverse premiums, tenant incentives, bad debts, negative growth and over-rented properties.[8]

References

1 Davidson, A.W. *Parry's Valuation and Investment Tables*, 12th Edition, Estates Gazette, 2002 (1st Edition 1913).
2 Rose, J.J. *Property Valuation Tables*, Freeland Press, Oxford, 1976.
3 Bowcock, P. *Property Valuation Tables*, Macmillan, 1978.
4 Bornand, D. 'Quarterly in advance closely observed', 275EG690.
5 Barham, R. 'The client's true interests?' 261EG129.
6 Mackmin, D. 'How effective are tables?' 259EG23.
7 Bornand, D. 'Compounding confusion', 282EG20.
8 French, N. 'Editorial: Market Values & DCF', *Journal of Property Valuation and Investment,* Vol. 12, No. 1, 1994, pp. 4-6.

Further Reading

Bornand, D. 'Year's Purchase Closely Observed', 273EG580.
Bornand, D. 'Between Agreement and Completion', 274EG790.
Cissell, R. and H. *The Mathematics of Finance*, Houghton Mifflin, 1973.
Enever, N. 'The Valuation of Investments – Which Tables?' *Estates Gazette,* June 1976, p. 864.
Mackmin, D.H. 'Quarterly in Advance', 276EG604.
Rose, J.J. *Construction of Valuation Tables*, The Incorporated Society of Valuers and Auctioneers.

Chapter Seven

Rack-Rented Freeholds

Investment Method of Valuation

In essence, the *investment method of valuation* involves the following calculation:

$$\text{Net income} - \text{years' purchase} = \text{capital value}$$

where net income is constant.

Net income will be constant for the period of years for which it is fixed in the lease. If the lease happens to be of land without buildings on a very long term with no rent reviews and the interest to be valued is the freehold, then there could be little argument that the application of the investment method of valuation would be correct. The investment being freehold land, would be assumed to produce a perpetual income and the rent being fixed under a long lease would be assumed to be perpetually constant, and could thus be capitalised using the *years' purchase* in perpetuity. An extremely simple example is now given to illustrate various points at this stage.

Example 7.1

Value the freehold interest in land let on a ground lease for 900 years unexpired at a fixed rent of £1,000 per annum net. A similar investment but let to produce £1,500 per annum net has just been sold for £7,500.

Stage 1: Analysis

Recent transactions involving comparable investments should be analysed to determine the market yield. As many good comparables as possible will be sought, but the more unusual the investment the fewer will be the comparables available. In this instance only one comparable is quoted, and this situation may indeed arise in practice in which event it is most important to ensure that this was a transaction 'at arm's length' or in other words a true reflection of market value with no special purchaser bid or other special circumstances. If there was a special purchaser, such as the occupier, then it would be reasonable to consider whether or not the occupier would be the most likely purchaser of the investment to be valued, in which case the client should be advised accordingly. In any event, with only one comparable available, the yield on analysis could be obliquely compared with yields on other investment opportunities, and the valuation generally considered from various viewpoints. In this example, the income being fixed for a long period might be comparable with the income from gilt-edged stock but the yield may be possibly higher to reflect proportionately higher costs of transfer and management. 'Does the yield fit in with this general picture?' is the question which should be asked.

Analysis:

$$\frac{\text{Net income}}{\text{Capital Value}} \times 100 = \text{yield}$$

$$\frac{\pounds 1,500}{\pounds 7,500} \times 100 = 20\%$$

Stage 2: Capitalisation

The income of £1,000 per annum is net of outgoings and therefore does not need to be adjusted. It is fixed for 900 years and any change in income which will occur after that is too remote to affect the valuation and therefore a YP in perpetuity can be adopted. The two investments are stated to be similar and therefore it may be reasonable to assume that the market would accept the same yield. The only noted difference between the two investments is their size, and it may be that the market would be prepared to accept a lower yield on the larger investment if the costs of transfer and management are proportionally lower for example. For the purposes of this exercise, however, the same yield is assumed.

Capitalisation:

Net income		£1,000 pa	
YP in perp.	$\dfrac{1}{0.2}$ =	5	
Capital Value		£5,000	

The investments quoted above are unusual, although it is fairly common to find ground leases of 99 years with reviews say every 33 years. The type of investment which valuers are frequently faced with, however, is the commercial property let on a FRI lease with frequent rent reviews, say every five years. In view of long experience of inflation, the most likely pattern of future income flow from such an investment may be an increase on each review into the foreseeable future. At some very long time into the future there may be a fall in income as the building reaches the end of its economic life, but this event is generally regarded as so remote as not to affect the valuation. How then are the likely increases in income in the foreseeable future to be reflected in the valuation? The traditional answer is that the capitalisation rate adopted will allow for any future income growth, provided that it is derived from an analysis of market yields of *comparable* investment transactions – and it is most important that these comparables should be similar with regard to lease terms permitting similar future increases in rent.

There follows a typical investment method valuation of a commercial rack-rented freehold investment.

Example 7.2

A modern office block is let on a full repairing and insuring lease for 25 years with reviews to the full rental value every five years, at a current rent of £75,000 per annum. Analysis of market data shows the current income to be the rack rental value and the acceptable yield for this type of investment to be 5.5%. Value the freehold interest.

Net income (FRV on FRI lease –		
management ignored as being reflected in the		
capitalisation rate)	£75,000 pa	
YP in perp. @ 5.5%	18.1818	
	£1,363,635	
Such a figure might be rounded to, say,	£1,360,000	

There is a school of thought which does not regard this method as being adequate and considers that the likely future income pattern should as far as possible be made explicit in the valuation. Such a procedure may, and in some cases must, be adopted in complex valuations involving leasehold interests and reversionary investments or subjective estimates of worth to an individual purchaser, and the following chapters examine these situations. It is the author's opinion, however, that in valuing simple rack-rented freehold investments, the traditional investment method is almost always a correct market approach and furthermore is logical, if one is prepared to accept the yield as an 'all risks' yield reflecting all risks and potentialities including the probability of future income growth.

The Limited Life of Buildings

As seen earlier the conventional method of valuing a freehold rack rented investment is to capitalise the income in perpetuity, ignoring as too remote the eventual reversion to site value upon the expiration of the economic life of the building. An alternative method might be to estimate the life of the building, and either allow in the valuation for rebuilding at the end of that time, or to assume that the rent attributable to the building will cease and that only a rent attributable to the site will continue. Even if it were possible to make a reasonable estimate of the life of the building, in most circumstances the reversion would be so distant as not to significantly affect the valuation. Thus, for example, if a building were assumed to have a life of 60 years and the YP 60 years @ 6% were adopted, this would produce YP of 16.1614 as against a YP in perp. @ 6% of 16.6, a difference of approximately 3% which would be reduced by adding in residual site value in the first calculation. The longer the period of deferment and the lower the rate of interest, the smaller the difference between the YP in perp. and the YP single rate becomes. This is because, through the process of discounting, greater weight is attached to cash flows produced earlier in the life of the investment, and the lower rates of interest imply lower time preference for early cash flows. A difference of 5%, which may be regarded as being significant between the YP in perp. and the YP single rate, is achieved at YP 62 years @ 5% or 22 years @ 15% for example.

For a modern freehold rack-rented investment in normal circumstances it is probably therefore reasonable not to make any specific allowance for the life of the building, but to allow this unquantifiable feature of the investment, amongst others, to be reflected in the discount rate. In the case of old buildings and high discount rates, however, the matter may be regarded as significant. But there are a number of problems associated with making explicit allowance for termination of the economic life of the building.

To estimate the life of a building with any degree of precision is usually an impossible exercise. If the valuer looks to experience and information about the history of buildings for assistance, he will find difficulties of comparison because of the relative lack of evidence of long-term performance of some modern building materials and techniques and the changes taking place in society, possibly making buildings become obsolete more quickly than hitherto. Other problems include the difficulty of allowing for changes in rebuilding costs between now and the end of the life of the building and of determining a basis upon which to estimate the rent appropriate to the site of the building which might hold good until the end of the building's life.

In view of these problems, it is suggested that making such explicit allowances is only applicable where redevelopment is due to take place in the foreseeable future, and in these circumstances it might be thought appropriate to capitalise the term income on either a dual rate or a single rate basis.[1]

Taxation

The Income and Corporation Taxes Act 1970 provides for the taxation of income derived from real property. In general, rent from unfurnished property is taxable in accordance with Schedule A. There is provision in this Schedule for such matters as deductions in the form of allowable expenditure; provisions for 'spreading' heavy expenditure in one year, such as accrued dilapidations in certain cases; provision for apportionment of premiums between income and capital elements for tax purposes; and sundry other matters.

At the time of writing, the tax rates are as set out below, although these will obviously vary year by year.

Individuals

Income Tax for 2000/2001

£0–£1,520	@ 10%
£1,521–£28,400	@ 22%
Excess over £28,400	@ 40%

Capital Gains Tax for 2000/2001
Gains in excess of annual exemption taxed at income tax rates as top slice of income. The annual exemption is £7,200.

Companies

Corporation Tax for year ending March 31 2001 chargeable on income and capital gains

Full rate	30%
Small companies rate	20%

(Turnover between £50,000 and £300,000)

Taxation and Valuation

The foregoing is a very brief survey of taxation. The effects of taxation are of course relevant to property decisions. Vendors, purchasers, landlords and tenants should have regard to the taxation aspects of transactions. For example, the exact combination of rental and premium in granting a lease will have tax implications for landlord and tenant alike. Particularly intricate relationships may arise between the structure of a company and the transactions with which it is involved. An investment appraisal may have regard to capital allowances on industrial buildings and plant and machinery in offices and other commercial properties, and in Enterprise Zones.

These are generally matters of investment decision making, rather than valuation. The conventional approach to income tax in the valuation of freehold interests is that since investment income generally is subject to the same incidence of tax, yields may be quoted gross of tax for ease of comparison. In adopting this attitude, the property market is acting consistently with the stock market, the money market and the labour market, where yields (or wages) are quoted on a gross basis.

There are situations, however, where it might be appropriate to make allowance for tax in the valuation. The most obvious of these is the subjective (ie non-market) valuation for an individual investor who desires to know the value to him of an investment taking account of his particular tax position. In carrying out such a valuation, care will have to be had in considering the marginal effects of the transactions on his income or capital but in many cases such an appraisal will just not be possible with any degree of precision. It cannot be known, for example, whether a company will make a profit, and if so how much profit, in any particular tax year until well after the transaction being contemplated.

As regards market valuations, if tax is to be taken into account then the dominant investors in the market must be identified, and the more easily identifiable they are, the easier will be the tax adjusted valuation. In the case of a single potential purchase – and this would not always be regarded as a true market – there would be the tax effects on only one purchaser and one vendor to be taken into account. But even in this relative straightforward situation, problems would arise, always assuming all the relevant data was available. Such problems would include marginal tax rates, profit/loss forecasting, deferred payment of tax, etc. How much more difficult then would such an exercise be with a larger market? Perhaps the best that may be hoped for is that the most probable purchaser may be identified and the most probable effects on his tax affairs and those of the vendor will be identified. In the majority of cases, however, it is thought that a tax adjusted valuation is impractical and probably unnecessary.

In any event, in the case of rack-rented freeholds, provided the capitalisation rate derived from comparables is consistent with that used in the valuation, the answer will be the same whether the valuation is conducted on a gross-of-tax or net-of-tax basis.

Example 7.3

A freehold property let at the net rack-rent of £1,000 per annum has just been sold for £10,000. This represents a 10% yield thus:

$$\frac{1,000}{10,000} \times 100 = 10\%$$

This is the yield which the market is prepared to accept for a gross income of £1,000 per annum. What does this represent in terms of a net yield assuming tax at 40%?

Gross income	£1,000 pa
Less tax at 40%	400
Net income	£600

If this transaction is analysed on a gross basis, the yield is seen to be 10%; if on a net basis, 6%. If a similar property is to be valued on a net-of-tax basis, this net yield must be adopted in the capitalisation thus:

Gross income	£600 pa
YP perp. @ 6%	16.6
Capital value	£10,000

A net-of-tax valuation of a rack-rented freehold investment is therefore only necessary if the worth of an investment to a particular client is to be considered or the market can be sufficiently identified.

Example 7.4

What is the maximum price a non-taxpayer should pay for the above investment if he is prepared to accept the net-of-tax market yield?

Gross income	£1,000 pa
Less tax (N/A)	–
Net income	£1,600 pa
YP perp. @ 6%	16.66
Capital value	£16,600

If the non-taxpayer paid this amount for this investment, he would be receiving the same net yield as the 40% taxpayer. However, he would have completely bid away his consumer surplus. If the market value is £10,000, he is unlikely to have to pay in excess of that figure, and hence his net yield would be 10%. Alternatively, a compromise may be reached whereby the purchaser and vendor both share in the purchaser's tax advantage.

Tax-adjusted valuations of leasehold and reversionary investments are dealt with in the appropriate chapters.

DCF Analyses with Growth

Inflation and Real Value Changes

In the absence of inflation in the economy, an increase in the value of an investment would represent a true reflection of its increased value caused by changes in supply and demand. In an inflationary economy such real value changes can equally occur but are distinguishable from apparent increases in value which are in fact the result of a depreciation in the value of the currency.

In comparing fixed interest securities with equity-type investments, the former are said to be 'inflation prone' and the latter 'inflation proofed'. It would therefore be possible to deduct the current rate of inflation from the current yield on gilt-edged stock to make a comparison with equity yield, or a more complex appraisal could be undertaken which would involve forecasting inflation rates. However, equity-type investments including most properties are hedged against inflation to varying degrees and are therefore only relatively 'proofed' against inflation, although some may beat the rate of inflation. Undated gilts, on the other hand, are absolutely 'inflation prone' as the future return on these investments is known with certainty to be fixed. The practice has arisen therefore of using the yield on gilts as the fixed point of reference and adjusting the yields on equity-type investments upwards for anticipated value changes in making comparative appraisals. Alternative possibilities would be to analyse the recent performance of properties or property shares taking into account growth.[2]

For investment appraisal purposes, generally no distinction is made between real value changes and changes due to inflation in the economy, and this is the policy generally adopted in the appraisals contained in this book. Such undifferentiated changes in value are referred to as 'growth', even though some or all of that growth may only be truly so called in comparison with fixed interest securities (which in real terms are declining in value).

The Equated Yield

A DCF appraisal of a rack-rented freehold property may be carried out by reflecting anticipated growth in the future cash flows. The cash flows are thereby effectively made comparable with the income from fixed interest securities by being made explicit for a good part of the life of the investment. It is then only right to compare the discount rate with the yield obtainable on fixed interest securities. Tables suitable for such appraisals have been compiled, and those generally used in the appraisals contained in this book are *Donaldson's Investment Tables*,[3] although *Parry's* does now contain similar investment tables. These tables use the term 'equated yield' to define the discount rate contained in such appraisals. Some valuers prefer the term 'redemption yield' in this context and use the term 'equated yield' to define the discount rate contained in DCF appraisals of reversionary freeholds where growth is not built into the future cash flows, but these are not the definitions adopted herein.

There are four major variables in an equated yield analysis, and these are as follows:

(i)   The initial yield.
(ii) The annual growth rate of rental income.
(iii) The rent review period.
(iv) The equated yield.

In appraising a rack-rented freehold, the most usual circumstances will be as follows:

(i)   The property will be let and therefore the current income will be known. If it is not, then it can be estimated by the usual methods of comparison.
(ii) The purchase price will be known, in which case the initial yield can be determined by combining this information with that given at (i). If it is not known, then the property can be valued by the investment method of valuation, deriving the initial yield from market data.
(iii) The rent review period will be known, being contained in the lease, or can be derived from market data. In the case of prime investments it is currently likely to be five years.

With this information being known or estimated by traditional methods, there remain two unknown variables, viz (i) the annual growth rate of rental income, and (ii) the equated yield. This type of analysis can only reveal one unknown variable, in which case the other one needs to be estimated or derived from market data.

Table 7.1

Years (inclusive)	Amt £1 @ 12%	Expected rent (cash flow)[i]	Trial rate 16%[ii]			Trial rate 17%[ii]		
			PV £1 @ 16%[ii]	(Deferred) YP[iii]	Present Value of Tranche[v]	PV £1 @ 17%[ii]	(Deferred) YP[iii]	Present Value of Tranche[v]
1st–5th	N/A	£50,000	N/A	3.2743	£163,715	N/A	3.1993	£159,965
6th–10th	1.7623	£88,115	0.4761	1.5589	£137,362	0.4561	1.4592	£128,577
11th–15th	3.1058	£155,290	0.2267	0.7423	£115,272	0.2080	0.6655	£103,346
16th–20th	5.4736	£273,680	0.1079	0.3533	£96,691	0.0949	0.3036	£83,089
21st–25th	9.6463	£482,315	0.0514	0.1683	£81,174	0.0433	0.1385	£66,801
26th–30th	17.0001	£850,005	0.0245	0.0802	£68,170	0.0197	0.0630	£53,550
31st to perp.	29.9599	£1,497,995	0.0116	0.232[iv]	£347,535	0.0090	0.18[iv]	£269,639
Total Present Values					£1,009,919			£864,967
Less: outlay					£1,000,000			£1,000,000
NPV					+£9,919			–£135,033

$$IRR = 16 + \left[1 \times \frac{9,919}{144,952} \right] = 16.06$$

Notes

(i) The initial rent of £50,000 is multiplied by the Amount of £1 for the period up to the review at the expected growth rate. The relevant figure of Amt £1 is shown in the previous column.

(ii) These rates of interest are trials for the IRR (equated yield).

(iii) With the exception of years 31-perp., these deferred YPs are calculated by multiplying the YP 5 years @ 16% (3.2743) and 17% (3.1993) respectively by the PV £1 at the same respective rates for the period up to the review. The resultant figures represent the sum of the PVs for the appropriate period. The relevant figures of PV £1 are shown in the previous columns.

(iv) These figures are produced by multiplying the YP in perp. @ 5% (20) by the PV £1 for 30 years at 16% and 17% respectively. As growth has not been specifically allowed for in the cash flows after 30 years, it is allowed for by using the low initial yield rate to capitalise such future flows. Obviously the appraisal cannot continue indefinitely, and therefore a suitable 'cut-off' point has to be adopted. This and the capitalisation rate used at this point are discussed in the text.

(v) These figures are produced by multiplying the relevant cash flow by the appropriate (deferred) YP.

Analysing for Equated Yield

The following appraisal is undertaken manually in order to demonstrate the method. In practice this would be undertaken by reference to tables or (particularly where the data is beyond the scope of the tables) by computer or programmable calculator.

Example 7.5

A freehold rack-rented office investment producing £50,000 per annum net has just been purchased for £1,000,000. The lease is for 25 years with five-year reviews. Assuming 12% per annum growth in rental values, determine the equated yield.

The analysis is given at Table 7.1.

The procedure of adopting a 30-year 'cut-off' point and then capitalising at the initial yield rate follows the basis of calculation used in *Donaldson's Tables*. It is thought that to extend the analysis beyond 30 years would not produce a significant difference. However, it can reasonably be argued that it would be better to revert to an assumption of fixed income beyond a certain point in time in order to reflect obsolescence. This can be done by capitalising the remaining fixed income at the equated yield rate. Thirty years is probably normally too short a time for obsolescence to have such an effect, and if the fixed income assumption is made after so short a period it can make a significant difference to the result. The arguments have in fact been dealt with in an earlier section on the *limited life of buildings,* and in view of the conclusions drawn there, the basis of *Donaldson's Tables* is considered logical.

The equated yield in this example is found to be 16.06%. If this exceeds the investor's opportunity cost of capital rate, the investment will normally be regarded as worthwhile.

Analysing for Growth

An alternative way of analysing an investment would be to select a target equated yield and analyse for implied growth.

Example 7.6

A prime freehold rack-rented shop investment available for purchase offers an initial yield of 4.5% and rent reviews every five years. What annual rate of growth will be required to match the investor's long-term opportunity cost of capital rate of 14%.

Donaldson's Tables show that for a five-year review pattern at an initial yield of 4.5% and a growth rate of 10% per annum, the equated yield is 13.7%, whereas for a growth rate of 11% per annum, the equated yield is 14.71. These results may be tabulated as follows:

Growth rate % pa	Equated Yield %	Equated Yield – Target EY (14%) %
10	13.78	−0.22
11	14.71	+0.71

By linear interpolation the growth rate may then be calculated as follows:

$$10 + \left[1 \times \frac{0.22}{0.22 + 0.71} \right] = 10.237\% \text{ pa}$$

An alternative method of arriving at this answer would be by the use of the following formula:

$$\text{Growth rate pa} = \left[\sqrt[n]{1 + \frac{(E - 1)}{AF}} \right] -1$$

where
n   = number of years between reviews
E   = equated yield rate
I   = initial yield rate
AF = annual sinking fund for review period at rate E.

Hence in this example,

$$\text{Growth rate pa} = \left[\sqrt[5]{1 + \frac{(0.14 - 0.045)}{0.1513}} \right] -1$$

$$= 10.237\%$$

Yet a further possibility, and certainly the simplest where the required variables are available, would be to refer to *'Implied Growth Rate Tables'*[4] which provide sets of implied growth rate figures on both a 'yearly in arrears' basis and a 'quarterly in advance basis'.

Valuations by Equated Yield

A third aspect of the equated yield approach is the possibility of valuing freehold rack-rented investments.

The tables are most likely to be of assistance in this process where the two investments being compared have different rent review patterns.

Example 7.7

Value a freehold rack-rented property investment let on lease with five-year rent reviews and producing a net income of £30,000 per annum. The only suitable comparable, which is a virtually identical property, also produces an income of £30,000 per annum net, is let on lease with three-year rent reviews, and has just been sold for £650,000.

Steps to a Possible Solution

1. Determine the initial yield of the comparable as follows:

$$\frac{30,000}{650,000} \times 100 = 4.62\%$$

2. Determine the investor's opportunity cost of capital (EY) rate, say 16%.
3. From *Donaldson's Tables* find the initial yield for a five-year rent review pattern which corresponds with the initial yield of 4.62% for a three-year review pattern and 16% equated yield. The nearest corresponding set of figures is in fact for an EY rate of between 16.06% and 16.27% which may be regarded as sufficiently accurate given the inaccuracies inherent in determining an EY rate in the first place, and by interpolation the appropriate initial yield is found to be approximately 5.1%.
4. Value the subject property as follows:

Net income	£30,000 pa
YP @ 5.1%	19.6
Capital Value	£588,000

The above approach may, however, be regarded as slightly artificial. If a five-year review pattern is the norm then the market may regard with suspicion a rent of the same magnitude on a similar property let on a three-year pattern. Was the tenant in a weak bargaining position? If so, what of the strength of his covenant? If, on the other hand, a three-year pattern is the norm, is there an underlying strength in the covenant of the tenant who managed to negotiate a five-year review pattern at the same rent, which would tend to offset the effect of the mathematical approach adopted above? So again, mathematics may play only a small part in the valuer's approach to the problem. Aspects of this problem are developed further in Chapter 10.

Other circumstances in which valuers may decide to adopt the equated yield approach are in providing subjective valuations (or valuations to show the worth of a property to an individual), market valuations where there is no market evidence, or as a check on market valuations where market evidence is thin. In these cases it is the initial yield rate which is the unknown quantity. The opportunity cost of capital rate has to be estimated and the growth rate has to be forecast. Perhaps all that can be said in favour of this precarious procedure is that 'like the prospect of hanging, the attempt to formalise and make explicit can only concentrate the mind'.[5]

Example 7.8(a)

In the absence of all market evidence, value for accounts purposes a prime freehold rack-rented property investment producing £40,000 per annum net with reviews every five years. Undated gilts are yielding 15% and the estimated rate of rental growth is 10% per annum.

Assuming an EY rate of 18% (gilts plus a margin of 3 percentage points), *Parry's Tables* show that the initial yield corresponding to the above data is approximately 9.5%. The valuation would then proceed as follows:

Net income	£40,000 pa
YP @9.5%	10.53
Capital Value	£421,000

Perhaps the method may be used as a check on remote property market evidence, or on the other methods in determining a capitalisation rate to value special properties by the investment method, or immediately after a crash in the market where there is virtually no market. In the latter situation it would be a brave person indeed who would be prepared to forecast growth rates; Stock Market comparisons may also be unhelpful at such times. It could conceivably be used in statutory valuations where there is no market, as for example in valuations under the Leasehold Reform Act. This points up a conflict, however, between valuers who prefer evidence from the money market and those who prefer evidence from a virtually non-existent property market. The Lands Tribunal are known to prefer evidence from the direct property market rather than the money market, and may be prepared to look at 'evidence' far removed in both time and place from the transaction under consideration before looking at the money market.

The main difficulty is in forecasting a growth rate, and Part III seeks to provide some background to this problem. The effect of varying the growth rate can have significant effects on the valuations, however, as shown below.

Example 7.8(b)

Using the facts and assumptions other than the growth rate from example 7.8(a), value on the assumption of an 8% per annum growth rate.

Donaldson's Tables show the appropriate initial yield to be about 11.5%. Therefore the valuation is now as follows:

Net income	£40,000 pa
YP @ 11.5%	8.696
Capital Value	£348,000

This compares with an answer of £421,000 in Example 7.8(a), a significant difference achieved by varying the growth rate by only two percentage points. In normal circumstances, therefore, such methods must be regarded as prone to inaccuracy and indeed unnecessary in market valuations of rack-rented freeholds. However, they may have a role in determining the optimum bid of an individual purchaser or influencing the disposal policy of an investor.

The Yield on Gilts as a Measure of the Opportunity Cost of Capital

Most valuers would shy away from the idea of forecasting growth, but many would be prepared to discuss the appropriate *opportunity cost of capital (EY) rate*. When this is required for a subjective valuation, then borrowing costs, debt and taxation structure are all relevant. But where a more objective approach is required, the usual yardstick is the rate on undated gilts, for reasons already given. In the context of institutional investment this may be questioned for the following reasons:

(i) There is a need for portfolio diversification, and it is wrong to measure performance by reference to one sector of the portfolio only.

(ii) There are important qualitative differences between gilts and property.

(iii) The yield on gilts changes more rapidly than that on properties, the stock market being a far more fluid market. For this reason, if gilts are being used as a yardstick then a generalised view of gilt rates over a few months rather than the yield on a particular day, may be appropriate.

(iv) Institutions would not invest in undated gilts as an alternative to property. This is a fundamental criticism in the light of which comparison with dated stock yields suitably adjusted for the effects of taxation, may be more appropriate.

Before considering alternatives, the next question to consider is: if undated gilts are to be used as a datum, should a margin be added to produce an EY rate, and if so how much?

At one extreme it could be argued that in a NPV valuation, if the cash flows are indeed the best estimates thereof, then there is no reason to adjust the discount rate to allow for additional risk. But in estimating the growth inherent in the cash flows, the property investment is only made comparable with the gilt-edged stock in terms of being prone to inflation. The other differences remain.

Rather than explicitly comparing property with gilts to determine an EY rate, an alternative approach would be to use the rate acceptable in the market for best quality large fixed ground rents. Yet further aid in this direction may be obtained by calculating the overall return which has actually been achieved in recent years on property extrapolating this into the future. Further attention is given to these points in Part III.

References and Notes

1 For a further discussion see *Modern Methods of Valuation*, T. Johnson, K. Davies and E. Shapiro, Estates Gazette, 2000.
2 For a further discussion see 'The Evaluation of Cash' by Charles Ward (260EG253).
3 Marshall, P. *Donaldson's Investment Tables.*
4 Rose, J.J. *Implied Growth Rate Tables.*
5 Sloam, N.S. 'Individual Worth Approach', 255EG45.

Further Reading

Colborne, A. 'Tax Explicit Calculations: Industrial Building Allowances for the Small Investor', *Journal of Valuation*, Vol. 2, No. 2.
'Real Value Approaches', 279EG756.

Chapter Eight

Leasehold Interests

Introduction

Leasehold interests may be categorised in a number of different ways as follows.

(a) Very short leaseholds, say up to 10 years.
(b) Short leaseholds, say 10 to 25 years.
(c) Long leaseholds, say 25 to 100 years (although some commentators would also insert medium leaseholds, say 40 to 70 years).
(d) Very long leases, over 100 years and generally treated as freeholds for valuation purposes.

Leasehold interests may also be purchased for two independent reasons, viz: occupation or investment.

Profit Rent

For a variety of reasons a leaseholder may be paying a rent which is less than the full rental value of the premises or the rent which he is receiving if he has sublet. This would arise in the case of the leasehold developer who will merely pay a ground rent to the freeholder. It would also arise where the tenant paid a *premium* or carried out repairs upon entering into a lease in consideration of a reduction in the rent. A third possibility is that, in the case of an occupational lessee, property values may be rising continually, whereas the rent payable may be rising at intervals – the rent review periods, say five years; or in the case of an investor who has sublet, a similar situation may arise where he has sublet with a more frequent pattern of rent reviews than exist in the headlease.

Thus a leasehold interest may produce an investment income or it may produce a saving in rental payments to an occupational lessee. In either case the difference between the rent paid and the rent received or full rental value as the case may be (at the point of valuation) is termed a *profit rent*.

In calculating a profit rent it is important that the rent paid and the rent received or full rental value as the case may be are on the same basis with regard to outgoings or alternatively are notionally adjusted to put them on the same basis. For example, where a headlessee has taken on a full repairing and insuring lease but sublets on an internal repairing-only lease, then he retains responsibility for external/structural repairs and insurance, and the annual costs of these together with the annual costs of any management must be deducted from the rent received before the head rent can be deducted to arrive at a profit rent. Likewise if an occupational lessee has the benefit of an internal repairing only lease and all comparable evidence of rack-rented properties is on the basis of full repairing and insuring leases, then clearly the lessee would pay relatively more rent than if he had the burden of an FRI lease. In order, therefore, to arrive at a profit rent either the costs of external/structural repairs, insurance, and possibly some management must be added on to the estimate of full rental value on an FRI basis or deducted from the rent payable in order to put that on a net basis.

Where the full rental value or rent receivable is below the rent payable then there is a negative profit rent or *loss rent*. This may have a negative capital value in the market. In other words, a leaseholder in a loss rent situation may be prepared to pay a capital sum to a third party willing to take the interest off his hands a reverse premium. There may be very little evidence for such a procedure in the market, but in valuing a portfolio of properties it would be quite in order to place a negative valuation on such an interest as it clearly detracts from the overall value of the portfolio.

Capitalisation

A capital value may be placed on a profit rent and this is the purchase price of the investment, commonly termed a premium (although technically a premium is a capital sum paid on the granting of a lease), perhaps to reduce the level of rent.

The traditional method of valuing a leasehold interest is to multiply the profit rent by the years' purchase dual rate tax adjusted. This would be for the term of years over which the profit rent is receivable. Alternative methods of approach are considered later in this chapter. The cost of any *dilapidations* which are likely to be payable can be deducted as a lump sum from the purchase price.

The Accumulative Rate

In valuing on a dual rate basis it is necessary to determine an appropriate accumulative rate. The *raison d'être* of the dual rate approach is that at least some investors will seek to replace capital at low safe rates of interest (in the past possibly through leasehold redemption policies). The low rate of interest reflected the administrative costs of accepting and re-investing a succession of small payments and providing a guaranteed return over a long period and the guarantee of paying out a specified capital sum at a certain future date. The rate varies according to the length of lease in question. In practice, this method may be the only way of perpetuating the investment.

Where the investor pays income tax, then it may be appropriate to quote a net of tax accumulative rate. This represents the true return and the interest which is accumulating in the fund. Any money paid to the Inland Revenue obviously cannot accumulate in the fund and therefore cannot be reflected in the rate of interest quoted. A rate of interest commonly quoted is 3% net, which would for example on the basis of 25% income tax equate to 4% gross, although a slightly higher rate may be appropriate for short leases.

Some investors might still regard it as prudent to invest in a sinking fund policy, but most would not. 4% generally compares very unfavourably with rates on gilt-edged stock. An investor with short-term debt would clearly seek to service this at the current high rates of interest rather than to invest in sinking funds.

The Effect of Tax on Profit Rent

There are altogether three effects of income tax to be considered in valuing leasehold interests. Tax may be payable on the income received from the investment. If that income is to be divided between the true return on capital (*spendable* income) and that part which is to be set aside in a sinking fund, then the effects of taxation on each of these elements of income represent two facets of the problem. The third relates to the income tax, if any, payable on the interest receivable on the sinking fund investment. This third aspect was dealt with in the preceding section.

It has been noted elsewhere in this book that the normal basis of comparison between investments is on a gross of tax basis and hence gross of tax income and gross of tax yields are normally quoted. This applies to leasehold interests in so far as the spendable portion of the income is concerned. Where it may not be appropriate, however, is with regard to the part of the income set aside for recoupment of capital. If sinking fund instalments are indeed to replace capital then clearly they must come out of net of tax income.

There are two ways of dealing with this problem both with the same result. One is to carry out a net of tax valuation and the other is to use a years' purchase dual rate where the sinking fund element is grossed up to offset the effect of taxation.

The formula for the years' purchase dual rate adjusted for tax is as follows:

$$\frac{1}{i + s \, T_G}$$

where T_G represents $\dfrac{1}{1-x}$ where x is the rate of tax.

This T_G is known as the tax grossing up factor.

Where the net of tax approach is adopted, a net remunerative rate must be adopted and there is no need to gross up the sinking fund element as this also is to be treated net. Hence dual rate tables unadjusted for tax are appropriate in such a situation.

Example 8.1

Office premises A are let for £4,000 per annum with landlord responsible for external repairs, insurance and management. Premises B, which are similar, have just been let for £5,000 per annum on a full repairing and insuring lease. In the case of premises A there is a review to full rental value in four years' time. Value the leasehold interest in A.

Rent of B as applied to A pa		£5,000
Plus: landlord's outgoings:		
External repairs	say £500	
Insurance	say £200	
Additional management costs[i]	say £120	£720
Full rental value (in accordance with lease terms)		£5,720
Less rent paid under lease		£4,000
Profit rent pa		£1,720
YP[ii] 4 years @ 8% and 4% (tax 25%)		2.538
Capital Value		£4,365

Notes
(i) Some valuers ignore this item.
(ii) Derived from market data in practice.

Alternative Approach

Profit rent pa	£1,720
Less: tax @ 25%	£430
Net-of-tax income	£1,290
YP 4 years @ 6%[(i)] and 4% (no tax adjustment)	3.384
Capital Value	£4,365

Note
(i) 8% gross rate adjusted for tax at 25%.

That this answer will produce the required yield on capital and also replace capital is demonstrated below.

Capital to be replaced	£4,365
× asf 4 years @4%	0.2355
	£1,028
	£1,028
Net-of-tax income	£1,290
Less asf instalment	£1,028
Spendable income	£262

Yield (net-of-tax) $\dfrac{262}{4,365} \times 100 = 6\%$

One major problem in valuing by the traditional method is the selection of an appropriate tax rate. This problem would still arise on a single rate basis if carried out net-of-tax (see on p. 125).

The answer is to look at the sector of the market most likely to be bidding for the particular property and to take a view about the typical tax position of such potential purchasers. For example generally the institutions (mainly the pension funds and insurance companies) may be the only potential purchasers for the particularly large investments. The tax position of the institutions is known – pension funds and insurance companies have a somewhat complicated tax situation.[*] In this instance it would be possible to value on a gross-of-tax basis (which in the above example would include the use of a 5.3%[†] sinking fund) but the institutions would hope to see a relatively high return so that any tax advantage was not totally eroded. As a check, valuations for pension funds are sometimes carried out on a dual rate tax-adjusted basis. Subsequent analysis based on the true assumption

---

[*]For a further consideration of this see Chapter 13.
[†]$4\% \times T_G (1.3) = 5.3\%$

that no tax will be payable shows far higher returns than the remunerative rate adopted in the dual rate YP. Such an approach is only really logical when there are likely to be some taxpayers also in the market. Otherwise an unadjusted YP at a very high remunerative rate might as well be used in the first place. In any event, the answer will be the same and the relatively low capital values produced will reflect the relative unattractiveness of leasehold investments.

When the individual or a company is the most likely purchaser for a particular investment then the rate of tax to be adopted in such valuations is far more problematical. Even if a subjective valuation were to be carried out for an individual person or company, problems would arise as seen in the previous chapter. Even with accountant's advice it is not possible to arrive at a precise answer and therefore a generalised view must be taken. If it is considered that it is the taxpayer's average rate of tax which is appropriate, evidence shows that very few companies pay full corporation tax in view of losses, low profits, capital allowances and various reliefs.[1] Most individuals so arrange their tax affairs that their average tax rate is also fairly low. In such circumstances to adopt rates as high as 25% or 40% may be unrealistic, although this would be appropriate if, as seems more likely, the marginal rate of tax is considered more important.

The Remunerative Rate

In a fluent and open market of all types of leasehold investment, a pattern of years' purchases appropriate to different qualities of leasehold investments could be built up. Unfortunately in reality this is not the case, and the valuer may be left with few comparables of similar types of investment. It is therefore important for him to realise in what ways leasehold investments may differ from one another, and in the absence of any reliable leasehold comparisons he may have to look for evidence from the freehold investment or money markets.

In comparing with freeholds, it is first important to realise that leaseholds are top slice investments. The relationship between top and bottom slice investments is illustrated in Figure 8.1.

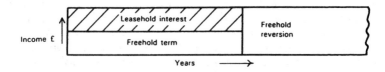

Figure 8.1

Here the profit rent shown shaded represents about 50% of the full rental value. Thus, if rental values fall, this income is quickly eaten into and a fall of as much as 50% would eliminate it altogether. It is thus very risky. On the other hand, the bottom slice, freehold term income, would remain immune to such a reduction in value. In the aftermath of a slump it is probably justified to regard top slice investments therefore with great suspicion. On the other hand, if rental values rise in the future, the *gearing* effect of such investments gives them a faster growth rate in the short term than freehold investments. The profit rent of an occupational lessee for example may rise from nothing to a substantial figure towards the end of the rent review period. A head leasehold interest subject to a fixed head rent will also show high growth during the currency of the lease. The deduction of a fixed sinking fund instalment from the income enhances the gearing effect. The relationship of the growth in rental income during the currency of leases involving different types of leasehold interest is illustrated in Figure 8.2.

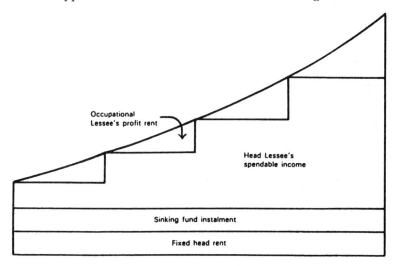

Figure 8.2

As regards comparison of capital values, in an inflationary economy the freehold capital value will increase perpetually (subject to the need to rebuild periodically) whereas leasehold interests are inherently wasting assets. However, the value of a leasehold interest can rise in the short term and only fall near the end of the lease. When plotted graphically a parabolic shape is produced. Very short leaseholds on the other hand may never increase in value but only diminish.

Comparison between leasehold and freehold remunerative rates is illogical in that if for the leasehold a sinking fund is set up, this will only replace historical capital, whereas a freehold investment will have an enhanced value after the same period of time in an inflationary economy. The comparison would be relevant in a non-inflationary economy because the sinking fund would perpetuate the investor's capital, making the leasehold comparable with the freehold, and the yield in terms of spendable income to capital value ratio between the two forms of investment would therefore also be presumed to be comparable. A slight upward adjustment in the case of the leasehold would be justified on grounds of the top slice effect and the restrictive nature and inherent disadvantages of the leasehold. In an inflationary economy, short leaseholds are probably more comparable with dated stock in terms of retaining a relatively static capital value profile on the basis of the traditional sinking fund approach. The difference would be that the income from the leasehold investment could fluctuate during the period of the lease whereas the income from the stock would remain constant. In both cases there could be short-term fluctuations in capital value.

It would be possible to devise an index-linked sinking fund but this moves away from the traditional concept of a sinking fund and might be more properly regarded as a part of overall investment or re-investment policy by the investor. Various methods have been proposed to allow for the effect of inflation on capital replacement, but most of these are probably impracticable. For example, if the required capital replacement figure is inflated by means of estimating a growth rate, and recoupment of this is provided by means of equal annual sinking fund instalments, then these instalments may exceed the profit rental income from the investment. The alternative would be to invest in a growth or high-yielding sinking fund although again it is difficult to describe these as sinking funds in the traditional sense. Such possibilities include investment in conventional gilt-edged stock or index-linked gilts. This, however, involves the problems of the continual need to invest small lots, the variation of the rates of interest on gilts, and the relatively large incidental costs of investment which such a policy would entail.

One further point to consider in carrying out dual rate valuations is the frequency and timing of sinking fund policy premiums. These are normally paid annually in advance. They can be paid quarterly or monthly in advance but the evidence suggests that they are never paid in arrear.[2] This therefore conflicts with the straightforward use of traditional tables where a valuation on the assumption of a sinking fund policy is to be adopted.

The Single Rate Basis

To overcome these problems associated with a sinking fund, it would be possible to value leasehold interests on a single rate basis. The single rate YP does after all allow for the replacement of capital albeit at the remunerative rate. If the investor is a taxpayer, it would still be necessary to value on a net-of-tax basis. Net-of-tax and gross-of-tax valuations only equate to one another when the income is perpetual. In valuing a profit rent valuation on a single rate basis, using an initial all-risks yield might be appropriate provided that the gearing effect and likely growth profile or otherwise of the investment is taken into account. Alternatively a DCF basis might be adopted.

By valuing on a single rate basis there would be an underlying assumption that the investor is prepared to put his capital fully at risk and could re-invest in further leaseholds or freeholds and hence perpetuate the investment portfolio. It would be easier to analyse a given YP as only two variables would be involved at the most, namely the remunerative rate and the tax rate where appropriate.

Other arguments against the dual rate approach are that for an occupational purchaser he may regard the acquisition of a short period of profit rent as payment of rent in advance rather than an investment; he is liable to be in occupation for longer than the profit rent period; his initial capital outlay may be by means of overdraft to be recouped out of profit – in all events a sinking fund would not be adopted. Secondly, as regards investors, and as has already been shown, investments can be made perpetual by continual acquisition of small investments in a portfolio. Thirdly, borrowers in either category will have a cost of capital well in excess of conventional accumulative rates and would therefore seek to reduce debt rather than invest in sinking fund policies.

In general, therefore, it may be said that the dual rate approach is no longer valid, it is understood to be virtually confined to the UK, and a recommendation for its general abandonment would seem to be in order.

The DCF Basis

In the foregoing methods the choice of remunerative rate may present considerable problems in complex leasehold valuations. An alternative is a true DCF approach. This does require a choice of discount rate and growth rate but at least it may be possible to derive these from the investment market generally, and the method does have a clear advantage of taking explicit account of the timing and effect of income changes.

Example 8.2

Value a head leasehold investment with nine years unexpired where the head rent is currently £10,000 per annum net and the rent from the sublessee has just been reviewed to £50,000 per annum net. The rent receivable is reviewable to full rack rental value every three years. The rent payable is reviewable to 30% of the rack rental value after three years but not thereafter. Assume a notional 'market' tax rate of 30%.

Valuation by DCF

First 3 years

Rent received		£50,000	pa net
Less rent paid		10,000	
Profit rent		£40,000	
Less: tax @ 30%		12,000	
Net of tax income		£28,000	
YP 3 years @ 12%[(i)]		2.4018	£67,250

Next 3 years

Initial rent received £50,000			
× Amount of £1 3 years @ 10%[(ii)]	1.331	£66,550	
Less: rent payable			
(30% new rack rent)		19,965	
		£46,585	
Less: tax @ 30%		£13,976	
New net-of-tax income		£32,610	
YP 3 years @ 12%	2.4018		
× PV £1 3 years @ 12%	0.7118	1.7096	£55,750

Last 3 years

Initial rent received £50,000			
× Amount £1 6 years @ 10%	1.7716	£88,580	
Less: head rent			
(remains fixed)		£19,965	
		£68,615	
Less: tax @ 30%		20,585	
		£48,030	
YP 3 years @ 12%	2.4018		
× PV £1 6 years @ 12%	0.5066	1.2168	£58,442
			£181,442
		say	£181,000

Notes
(i)   This corresponds to about 17% gross of tax (@ 30%), and must be a fixed interest rate, eg gilts plus a margin, or large best quality fixed leasehold ground rent rate.
(ii) This is the anticipated growth rate possibly derived from analysis of freehold transactions on an equated yield basis.

A more sophisticated DCF approach might take into account, for example, management costs and rent review fees on reviews and renewals.

The conventional method of approach would have been to present this as an initial net-of-tax income unchanged and capitalised for nine years. It is submitted that it would have been an extremely tricky exercise in the absence of considerable market data to select an appropriate remunerative rate to capitalise on either a single or dual rate basis. The following analysis merely shows the remunerative rates which would have to be used were this valuation carried out on a single rate or dual rate basis to produce the same answer. It would be somewhat coincidental if these rates were actually chosen.

It is an important theme of this book that there are no panaceas. Evidence from the market is the best basis from which to value, but in the absence of much evidence or where the evidence is difficult to analyse accurately a variety of approaches may need to be adopted.

Analysis to determine remunerative rate on a conventional valuation basis

Capital value	£181,000
+ initial net-of-tax income	28,000
Years' Purchase (for 9 years)	6.48

From the figures in the body of the tables it will be seen that this corresponds to a remunerative rate of about 7.1% (net-of-tax) on a *single* rate basis, or about 5.6% and 3% (net-of-tax) on a *dual* rate basis.

Other situations in which the DCF approach could be useful would be as follows:

1. To take account of precise timing of rental payment, for example head rent payable in advance, rent receivable under sublease payable in arrears;
2. To ascertain the premium which an incoming tenant might be prepared to pay in consideration of an abnormally long rent review pattern.

Alternative Approaches

Where there are complicated subleases, and an explicit DCF approach is not required, it might be possible to value firstly by capitalising the rents receivable incorporating any future changes, secondly capitalising the rent payable, and then deducting one capital sum from the other. If the head lessee is to bear outgoings in addition to the head rent then these could be capitalised separately and also deducted from the capitalised rents receivable. In carrying out these calculations it is likely to be considered that the rents receivable should be capitalised at a relatively high yield to reflect their comparative insecurity and that the rent and outgoings payable should be capitalised at a relatively low yield to reflect the obligatory nature of the commitment. Yet a further method of valuing these leaseholds which has been suggested is to firstly value the freehold in possession, secondly, value the freehold subject to the lease, and then deduct one from the other.[3]

Sundry Matters

There may be restrictions on alienation which seriously affect the valuation, such as for example, a clause requiring a tenant wishing to assign to first offer to *surrender back* his lease without consideration. This may, however, be restricted by the Landlord and Tenant Act 1954, Section 38. The tenant and his advisers must therefore make sure that a tenant who has to offer to surrender is entitled to receive proper payment for any value which may be in his lease at the time of the surrender together with fixtures and fittings and goodwill.

Provisos for *forfeiture on bankruptcy and liquidation* are provided in most leases. The effect of such a proviso on the valuation of a leasehold interest was examined in an article written under the auspices of the RICS and the Law Society and published in the *Chartered Surveyor*.[4] The legal issues involved are complex and it is only possible therefore to make very general statements in the present context. The legal and valuation problems divide themselves broadly into two categories: firstly where the lessee is not bankrupt, and secondly where he is bankrupt.

In the first category, a valuation may need to be made where a lease is to be assigned. In normal circumstances a prospective assignee will not regard the future possibility of his own bankruptcy as a factor affecting the valuation. As regards a valuation for subletting at a premium or for mortgage, however, there is the possibility that the head lessee will go bankrupt and therefore the extent to which this might prejudice the sublessee or mortgagee must be considered. By the Law of Property Act 1925 a sublessee or mortgagee may apply to the Court for relief from forfeiture, and although this is discretionary it seems reasonable to assume that if the person applying for relief is a person able to perform the covenants, relief would be granted. It may be appropriate, however, to reduce the valuation to reflect the possibility of incurring administrative costs in obtaining relief.

Where the lessee is bankrupt, the position of a sublessee or mortgagee is the same, but the position on assignment is different. By the Law of Property Act the trustees in bankruptcy have one year in which to assign a leasehold interest, after which there can be no relief from forfeiture.

The above general provisions as to relief from forfeiture do not apply to certain leases specified in the Law of Property Act, one of which is where the personal qualifications of the tenant are of importance. If the valuer is valuing for bankruptcy or where the possibility of bankruptcy or where the possibility of bankruptcy is to be borne in mind for any particular reason, it is suggested that reference is made to the Act and the article.

As regards *surrenders, renewals and extensions* of leases, when a lease is nearing its end, the lessee and possibly the lessor, may consider it desirable to agree arrangements for the future. Such an arrangement could take one of the following forms:

(i) The lease is surrendered and a new one is granted immediately. This makes the future secure for both parties. However, the lessee may be enjoying a profit rent under the current lease and he would clearly not wish to give this up without consideration from the lessor. Such consideration could take the form of a rent reduced below the full rental value under the new lease, and the amount of such reduction can be calculated from the point of view of both the lessor and the lessee by valuing their interests subject to the existing arrangements and then comparing these valuations with valuations made subject to the proposed arrangements.

(ii) There is a surrender and renewal, but the new lease is at the existing rent, or an agreed adjustment is made subject to the payment of a premium.

(iii) The existing lease is extended, in which case it is likely to be at the full rental value.

The Landlord and Tenant Acts 1927 and 1954 have made alterations to the landlord and tenant relationship in regard to business premises and many calculations relating to premiums, virtual rents, surrenders, renewals and extensions of leases should take into account the provisions of these Acts.

Briefly, the main provisions in this context are as follows:

(i) *Landlord and Tenant Act 1927*
   If the tenant carries out improvements which were not covenanted for in the lease, then provided he goes through the necessary statutory procedure, he is entitled on quitting to obtain compensation from his landlord for those improvements amounting to the lesser of their cost at the end of the lease or their value to the landlord.

(ii) *Landlord and Tenant Act 1954*
      At the end of his existing lease a tenant may be entitled to a
      new lease at the full rent but ignoring the value of any
      improvements he has carried out during the currency of the
      existing lease or the previous 21 years. There are certain
      grounds on which the landlord can obtain possession,
      however, and in some of these cases the tenant is entitled to
      compensation for disturbance.

The provisions of the Landlord and Tenant Acts and the detail of
the calculations which may be required on the surrender and
renewal or extension of a lease are lengthy and complex and
considered to be specialisations in themselves and accordingly
beyond the scope of this book.

However, one matter that should be given attention in these
types of calculation is the question of taxation. For example, the
effect on the tax affairs of a company by way of tax relief on
payment of a premium might affect their attitude. Reference in this
context should be made to the Income and Corporation Taxes Act
1988. It is important to remember that surrenders and renewals are
one of those areas where the attitude of the market is not the sole
criterion of valuation. It is one of those calculations like marriage
valuations* which concern two parties only and are therefore
intimately bound up with their business and taxation affairs in
general.

Key Money

One final item which should be mentioned in this chapter is the
question of *key money* payable by retailers to secure a prime pitch.
This is said to be payable for the right to trade notwithstanding the
fact that full rack rental value will be payable under the lease. This
makes for further difficulties in the analysis of data, as in analysing
a purchase price or premium a valuer needs to know how it is
made up – what constitutes key money, payment for good will,
payment for fixtures and fittings, and what represents the
capitalised profit rent. It is for this reason that the analysis of
leasehold transactions is difficult and it is necessary to separate
those transactions which are for investment purposes only and in
respect of which the premium represents capitalised profit rent
only, and those transactions which relate to occupational lessees.
These problems of analysis exist quite apart from the problems of
determining the constituents of a dual rate tax-adjusted YP. These

*Dealt with in Chapter 13.

factors all point to the need for clear thinking on the part of the valuer in analysing market data and/or analysing or valuing using DCF techniques.

It might be possible in some prime shopping streets for evidence of premiums paid to be built up. Such premiums inevitably include a major element of key money. It has been argued that notwithstanding the lack of logical justification for key money, such premiums should be regarded as market valuations of the interest concerned. In valuing for security purposes, of course, an indication should be made of the ephemeral nature of such premiums. It has been argued that payment of key money reflects the proposed security of tenure (including the disregards of assessing rent on review and renewal) afforded by the Landlord and Tenant Acts. In some quarters it is suggested that this should be devalued in calculating market rents. Conversely, it is sometimes suggested that open market lettings in such prime retail pitches may include an element in the rent bid of rentalised key money.

Conclusion

Study papers were produced as a follow up-to the Trott report.[5]

The main findings not already covered herein were as follows.

A purchaser for *occupation* acquiring a very short profit rent, say under 5 years, is likely to adopt a single rate approach or possibly DCF. Such a purchaser when acquiring a profit rent for say 5 to 25 years is likely to use the dual rate approach unadjusted for tax where there is a good demand for the investment.

A more conservative approach might be adopted where the demand is poor and a tax-adjusted YP would be considered appropriate. For 25 to 50 year profit rent, a tax-adjusted YP would generally be used.

It may be possible for a purchaser to arrange a sinking fund with tax relief, in which case use of non-adjusted tables would be appropriate. In addition, there are two matters of a capital nature which must be taken into account in carrying out a valuation for a prospective occupational purchaser. These relate to tenants' improvements and dilapidations. The effect of the latter would form part of the negotiations for the purchase. With regard to the former, the question must be asked as to whether the improvements are of general value to incoming purchasers and if so, what is the life of these improvements?

As concerns the acquisition of *short leaseholds for investments*, the question of dilapidations may become more important and may justify a relatively high yield. The effects of service charges and gearing must also be taken into account.

There is a relatively restricted market for short leaseholds for investment. The number of operators is small and in view of the competition in the market, they are fairly secretive about their methods. Theoretically it is considered that a single rate net of tax approach is advisable in respect of a taxpayer although a DCF approach is the best method. With regard to this type of investment, the use of quarterly in advance tables to accurately reflect the income flow becomes more significant.

It appears that in practice a number of different methods are used by valuers in valuing this type of investment. It is sometimes argued that this is of no consequence provided there is consistency between valuation and analysis ('as you analyse so shall you value'). Nonetheless it does appear to be significant that 51% of the valuers interviewed considered that leaseholds were generally incorrectly valued. This certainly suggests some confusion as to the correct techniques to be employed. For the record, the majority of valuers favour the dual rate unadjusted approach with a remunerative rate derived from gilts or comparable leaseholds (not adjusted from freehold yields), a 4% accumulative rate and an assumption of income annually in arrears. The latter two points appear mainly to be ones of convenience in that older editions of *Parry's* did not cover alternative approaches. *Parry's* is sometimes regarded as the Valuer's Bible and fortunately the current editions have been brought into line with recent thinking with regard to quarterly in advance tables.

Attention is now turned to *long leaseholds*. There are a small number of these in the market compared with freeholds partly due to the fact that they may be merged with freeholds and never come onto the market. It is suggested that when comparing with freehold yields there should be a mark-up determining the appropriate leasehold rates but this will be very low (possibly 0.25%) where the lease has approximately 100 years unexpired, rising to say 5 percentage points where the lease is considerably shorter (say 15 to 25 years). It is also shown that a conventional valuation is generally most sensitive to changes in the tax rate inserted rather than equivalent changes in the remunerative or accumulative rates for example. This emphasises the importance for the valuer in determining whether or not to use tax-adjusted tables. As has been shown, however, the consensus generally is for the use of non-tax adjusted tables when valuing for prospective investors.

References

1 *Treasury's Economic Progress Report*, April 1981.
2 Barham, R. 'Ever had that sinking (fund) feeling', 261EG219.

3 McIntosh, A.P.J. 'Valuing Leasehold Interests', 265EG939.
4 Gilchrist Smith, J. *Chartered Surveyor*, 1976.
5 Papers for the Valuation Techniques Seminar RICS/Polytechnic of the South Bank, February 1986:
   Department of Land Management University of Reading, *The Valuation of Short Leaseholds for Investment*.
   Edward Erdman incorporating views of Hillier Parker May and Rowden and Healey & Baker, *Short Leaseholds for Occupation*.
   Weatherall Green & Smith, *Long Leasehold Valuation Topic*.
   Polytechnic of Central London, *Net of Tax Valuations for Freeholds and Leaseholds*.

Further Reading

Aarons, L. 'Retail Lettings: Key Money or Opportunity Value', EG Issue 8838.

Boston, C. 'Making Sense of Key Money', 284EG20.

Fraser, W.D. 'The Valuation and Analysis of Leasehold Investments in Times of Inflation', 244EG197.

Ward, C. 'The Capitalisation of Negative Profit Rents', *Journal of Valuation*, Vol. 2, No. 2.

Chapter Nine

Reversionary Investments

Term and Reversion

Where a property is let below the full rental value and there is a prospect within the foreseeable future of a reversion to the full rental value then this type of investment is termed *reversionary*. There are two main approaches to the valuation of reversionary investments. The first of these is the *term and reversion* method sometimes known as the *block income* approach. This method involves capitalising the whole of the income in each tranche. The alternative method is known as the *hardcore/marginal* approach, sometimes referred to simply as the *hardcore* method or the *layer* approach. This approach entails capitalising the continuing income and separating from this the additional income which will arise on reversion and capitalising and deferring this.

As already noted, *top slice* income is traditionally regarded as less secure than bottom slice income. Hence a property let below the full rental value was traditionally regarded as a secure investment in that the tenant would be unlikely to default. In an inflation-free economy, if rack-rented properties of a particular type are selling to show a 5% yield then it might be reasonable to suppose that the term income of a reversionary investment should be capitalised slightly below this rate, say 4.5%. This corresponds to the traditional idea introduced in the previous chapter of capitalising leaseholds (being top slice investments) at slightly above the freehold rack rent rate partly on grounds of their top slice nature. By the same reasoning, it would be reasonable to value by the hardcore method capitalising the bottom slice at just below the rack rent rate and the top slice at just above this rate.

One problem traditionally associated with the hardcore method is that there is plenty of evidence of rack-rented investments and hence the yields derived from transactions involving these can be used as the capitalisation rates in valuing the reversion in the term and reversion method, but there is no direct market evidence of capitalisation rates appropriate for the bottom and top slices of these investments if taken separately. It has also been argued that it is conceptually wrong to divide an income and to capitalise each part at a different rate whereas in fact it is the whole income that is at stake and must be capitalised at the one rate. This criticism applies to both methods. In fact, the term and reversion method seems conceptually better for a literal term and reversion, but the layer method perhaps reflects a truer picture of the situation with regard to an upwards-only rent review. In this case the tenant has contracted to pay the lower layer of rent for the duration of the lease whereas the top slice is not so certain and in some circumstances may be regarded as a higher risk. Such a concept seems to have found favour in the property slump of the early to mid-1970s. In valuing a literal term and reversion by the traditional method it is possible to build in a void period following the expiry of the existing lease, if deemed appropriate in the circumstances. In a falling market where the income on reversion is predicted to be below the full rental value, then the layer method may be appropriate, using a high rate on the top slice of the term income, possibly also treating it as a terminable income valued on a dual rate basis.

Various methods have been proposed to overcome the problem of determining the relevant capitalisation rates in the use of the hardcore method. One of these is that a preliminary calculation should be carried out to determine the yield on the marginal income. This is done by capitalising the whole income at the appropriate rack rent rate and then deducting from this the capitalised value of the hardcore income at a rate somewhat below the rack rent rate, in both cases capitalising in perpetuity. The difference represents the capital value of the marginal income in perpetuity which when divided into that income produces the yield required on it. Such yield can then be used in valuing the marginal income by the hardcore method. By such a procedure the two methods should then be made to produce the same answers.

Having valued a reversionary investment by either method, the investor may require to know the overall yield. This will not be apparent from the valuation if more than one rate is involved. The overall yield may be regarded as the internal rate of return without building in any growth. This return is sometimes referred to as the *equivalent yield*. Until the advent of analysis for growth (now sometimes termed equated yield analysis), this yield was generally referred to as the equated yield. Some valuers still adhere to this meaning of the term. Any calculations involving the term equated yield should make clear whether this is with or without growth.

The following example shows two different methods of calculating the equivalent yield from a valuation where the interest rates used on term and reversion differ. Alternatively, the equivalent yield can be derived from graphs incorporated in *Donaldson's Investment Tables*. Where the interest rates used on term and reversion are the same then of course this rate will be the equivalent yield.

Example 9.1

A freehold factory is let for £10,000 per annum net on lease with four years unexpired. The full rental value is £30,000 per annum net. A valuation of the property is set out below. Calculate the equivalent yield.

Term			
Rent reserved	net pa	£10,000	
YP 4 years @ 8%		3.31	£33,100
Reversion			
FRV	net pa	£30,000	
YP reversion to perp. after 4 years @ 10%		6.83	£204,900
Capital Value			£238,000

(A) Solution by formula:

$$\frac{\text{Equivalent}}{\text{yield}} = \frac{(\text{Present income} + \text{annual equivalent of gain})}{\text{Price}} \times 100$$

$$\frac{\text{Annual equivalent of}}{\text{gain}} = \frac{\text{gain on reversion} \times \text{PV £1 for term}}{\text{YP for term}}$$

Gain on reversion = Value on reversion – price
Value on reversion (at current values) is as follows:

FRV	net pa	£30,000
YP perp. @ 10%		10
		£300,000

Gain on reversion = £30,000 – £238,000 = £62,000

Annual equivalent of gain = $\dfrac{£62,000 \times \text{PV £1 @ 9.5\%}^{(1)}(0.695)}{\text{YP 4 years @ 9.5\% (3.205)}}$

= £13,444

$$\text{Equivalent yield} = \frac{£10,000 + £13,444}{£238,000}$$

$$= \underline{9.85\%}$$

Note

(i) The rate of interest adopted for PV £1 and YP in calculating the annual equivalent of the gain should be the equivalent yield rate. As it is not known at that stage, an approximation has to be made. The calculation should then be repeated at different rates until the rate used at that stage corresponds to the equivalent yield rate. In this example, recalculations could therefore be made, using say 9.6% and 9.7%.

(B) Solution by DCF

Years	Cash flow	YP 9%	PV 9%	PV	YP 10%	PV 10%	PV
11–4	£10,000 pa	3.2397		£32,397	3.1699		£31,699
4	£300,000		0.708	£212,400		0.683	£204,900
				£244,797			£236,599
Less price				£238,000			£238,000
NPV				+ £6,797			£1,401

By linear interpolation,

$$\text{IRR} = 9\% + \frac{6,797}{6,797 + 1,401}$$

$$= 9\% + 0.83$$

Equivalent yield (IRR) = $\underline{9.83\%}$

Notes

1. As cash flows (instalments of income) for the first four years are constant, the YP for four years (ie PV £1 per annum) is adopted.
2. The cash flow of £300,000 in year 4 represents the value of the property on reversion. An alternative way of carrying out this part of the calculation is to capitalise the cash flow of 30,000 per annum by multiplying it by the YP reversion to perpetuity at the trial IRR rate.
3. This method avoids the degree of trial and error which may be necessary in using the formula method.
4. If a disposal is anticipated on or after reversion, the gain on reversion may be subject to capital gains tax. The effect of taxation could be built into the DCF solution if a net-of-tax appraisal is being undertaken.

The above somewhat long-winded calculations are merely an aid to the investor in enabling him to compare yields on rack-rented investments with the overall returns on reversionary investments. The equivalent yield concept in reverse is to use the freehold rack-rent rate or an appropriate variation thereon in valuing both term and reversion or valuing both layers of income by the hardcore method. The rate so used is properly termed the equivalent yield rate and does in fact ensure that valuations produced by either method result in the same answers. This particular approach is now finding favour amongst many valuers. It is adopted in the following example which illustrates the two methods. Further illustration is provided in Figure 9.1 which follows the example.

Example 9.2

In 1989 value the freehold interest in a factory built and let in 1957 on a 42-year lease with 14-year rent reviews on FRI terms. The current rent passing is £60,000 pa net. The premises comprise 18,000 sq ft of net lettable floor space. Similar premises are currently letting at £5 per sq ft FRI. 10% is considered an appropriate equivalent yield rate (similar but rack-rent investments produce 8.5% yield).

Estimation of FRV
18,000 sq ft at £5 = £90,000

Term and Reversion Method
Term

Net income	pa	£60,000	
YP 10 years @ 10%		6.1446	£368,676

Reversion

Estimated FRV	pa net	£90,000	
YP reversion to perp. 10 years 10%		3.85543	£346,989
			£715,665
		say	£715,000

Hardcore Method
Hardcore

Net income	pa	£60,000	
YP perp. @ 10%		10	£600,000
Top slice			
Estimated 'uplift'	net pa	£30,000	
YP rev to perp. 10 years @ 10%		3.85543	£115,663
			£715,663
		say	£715,000

Additional Information

Initial yield	$\dfrac{60,000}{715,000} \times 100 = 8.4\%$
Yield on reversion	$\dfrac{90,000}{715,000} \times 100 = 12.6\%$

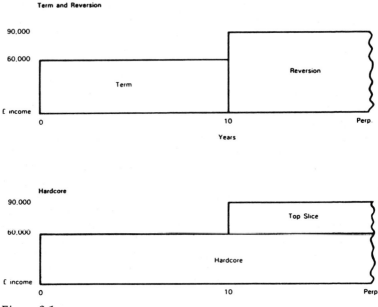

Figure 9.1

As regards the additional information provided, the investor will certainly be interested to know the initial yield and may be interested to know the yield on reversion. These valuations and yields have been calculated without regard to costs of transfer, although in practice these may be deducted from the valuation and this will marginally reduce the derived yields.

A reversionary investment will have an advantage to the investor increasing in magnitude according to his rate of tax on income. This is because the part of the capital value attributable to the increased income arising on reversion increases in value up to the reversion at the gross rate of interest applied in the valuation (this is disregarding any additional increase which may arise due to growth). As this increase in value is not received in the form of income it is not taxed as such.

In the above example the 10% capitalisation rate would need to have been derived from analysis of comparables. This type of reversionary investment is relatively rare and it is therefore likely that the valuer would need to make a judgement regarding the capitalisation rate as compared with yields obtained on rack-rented investments. The Polytechnic of Central London Study Report[2] in connection with the Trott Report[3] categorised reversionary investments as follows.

(a) Mildly reversionary, for example, three-, five- or seven-year reviews. These would constitute the majority of reversionary investments. They would be regarded slightly less favourably than rack-rented investments. They are unlikely to have much advantage for the high rate taxpayer. The capitalisation rate is likely to be marginally above the rack-rent rate, possibly 0.25 to 0.5 percentage points to reflect the possibility of an unfavourable rent review. Alternatively this matter could be dealt with by incorporating a conservative estimate of full rental value into the valuation.

(b) Highly reversionary investments involving a large rental uplift, say 300% or more. These will be in the minority comprising a diminishing group of old leases dating from the 1960s or earlier. This type of property has the disadvantage of age generally and refurbishment in the foreseeable future is liable to be necessary. This particularly applies to industrial properties. High yields are liable to result therefore. On the other hand, this type of investment will have advantages to the high rate taxpayer and this is liable to have a counteracting effect on the capitalisation rate adopted. At the end of the day, the rate used may well be similar to rack-rented investments.

A conceptual weakness of the approaches adopted in the above example or where the capitalisation rates are marginally varied according to the security in money terms, is that the degree to which the various tranches or layers of income are hedged against inflation is not explicitly reflected in the valuations. An alternative approach would be to regard the term income as similar to a fixed interest security and capitalise at an appropriate rate. The reversionary income would then need to be treated as a growth investment and capitalised either using an overall 'all risks' yield or by using an even more explicit DCF approach whereby the future income is enhanced to reflect anticipated value changes, is then capitalised at a rate appropriate to a growth investment, but discounted at a rate appropriate to a fixed interest security. This latter part of the procedure is needed to avoid 'double counting' the growth.

Term			
Net income	pa	£60,000	
YP 10 yrs @ 11.5%[i]		4.8765	£292,590
Reversion			
Estimated FRV	net pa	£90,000	
YP reversion to perp. after 10 yrs			
@ 9%[ii]		4.69345	£422,410
			£715,000

Alternative approach
Term

Net income	pa	£60,000	
YP 10 years @ 11.5%[i]		4.8765	£292,590

Reversion

Estimated FRV (current levels)	net pa	£90,000	
Amt £1 10 yrs @ 2%[iii]		1.219	
Estimated FRV (with growth)	net pa	£109,710	
YP perp. @ 8.5%[iv]		11.76	
Capital Value on reversion (allowing for growth)		£1,290,190	
PV £1 10 yrs @ 11.5%[i]		0.327	£422,410
			£715,000

Notes
(i)   This is a fixed interest rate. It may be derived from the rate on gilt-edged stock. It is arguable that no margin should be added because of the security of this income in money terms in that it is below the current rack rent. Alternatively, if evidence of fixed interest property investments can be obtained which would need to be of first-class type – if such are available – then these could provide a basis. Some valuers propound the theory that this term income valued on this basis should be capitalised on a dual rate approach, but the disadvantages of the dual rate concept have already been dealt with at length.

(ii)   This is the rack rent rate marginally adjusted upwards to reflect the uncertainty surrounding a future rent review as against the contracted rent situation which may pertain in the rack-rented comparables being analysed to produce a 9% yield. Again this matter is arguable.

(iii)   This is the anticipated growth rate and can be derived from equated yield analysis of rack-rented investments.

(iv)   This is the rack-rent rate. In this instance no margin is added because any additional risks are reflected in the higher rate adopted in the PV of £1 which follows.

The approach suggested above has come to be known as the short-cut DCF approach and the full calculation would involve the calculation of the growth rate used in the equation. For instance the growth rate can be calculated from the growth equation outlined in Chapter 7.

The growth rate pa =

$$\sqrt[n]{1 + \frac{E - I}{AF}} - 1$$

where
n   =   number of years between reviews
E   =   equated yield rate

I   =   initial yield rate
AF =   annual sinking fund for review period at rate E%
In the example
n   =   14
E   =   11.5% (this is the yield used for the term income and deferral)
I   =   8.5%
AF =   the annual sinking fund at 11.5%
thus the growth rate is 4.83%.

Another approach using what is termed as the implied growth rate formula is outlined later in the chapter.

Any method other than the explicit DCF model can be criticised on the grounds of placing too much reliance on the valuer's intuition as regards the extent to which the rack-rent rate should be varied to allow for a reversionary situation. Where there is, for example, only say two years to the next review, followed by a normal five-year review pattern, should not the equivalent yield be somewhat lower than the rack-rent rate to allow for the better prospects of growth than would apply with a normal rack-rented investment? If so, then the decision must be made as to what extent the yield should be varied. The more explicit DCF approach may also be considered desirable where there is the prospect of an uneven pattern of future growth, eg a relatively very low current income followed by a relatively very high one, or say a two-year period to review followed by a ten-year period, followed by a series of five-year periods.

Some help is at hand to the exponents of the equated yield method in the form of tables of rent adjustment factors to a five-year rent review pattern.[4] These show the necessary adjustment to the equivalent (or rack-rented) yield as the period to the next review increases from five years.

There are of course problems in the use of the more explicit DCF approach. Most of the rates of interest used in the above example are debatable. In the absence of any established pattern of valuations carried out on this basis and in the light of inability to analyse transactions to this degree of detail, these matters cannot be proved one way or the other. The Trott Report considered the term and reversion method preferable whereas the PCL research showed that the hardcore method was more commonly used in practice. Both theory and practice support the use of equivalent gross of tax yields. The possibilities of tax-adjusted valuations relating to both income tax and capital gains tax are considered later in this chapter, although in practice appear to be virtually unused. It is generally agreed that the equivalent yield method is theoretically sound in considering the investment as a whole rather than splitting it into term and reversion or top and bottom slices and regarding each as separate risks.

Theoretically, as has been shown, the term income on a reversionary investment is inflation-prone and it can be argued that the inflation-prone yield should be used to capitalise this tranche of income. In practice, this part of the investment is often fairly insignificant in value terms and accordingly this type of DCF approach finds little favour except possibly in the field of investment appraisal rather than valuation. The use of DCF, however, may be useful as a check particularly in the case of long reversions or short leaseholds.

Very high value reversionary investments are only likely to appeal to institutions. They will outbid the high rate taxpayers in many cases and the distortion of the market introduced by the latter group of investors will thereby be eliminated. Hope and marriage values may also have an effect on valuation of reversionary investments.

Parry's has tables of the internal rate of return with no projected rental growth. The analyst is able to ascertain this yield or rate of return by reference to the table provided he knows the initial yield and the uplift on the rent review or reversion. The latter presumably will need to be estimated by reference to market evidence.

Example 9.3

The purchase price of an investment is £250,000 and the initial income £10,000 per annum net. There is a reversion in five years' time to an estimated £20,000 per annum net with no projected rental growth. Ascertain the internal rate of return on this basis (or equivalent yield).

The rental factor is 2 (£20,000 divided by £10,000). The period to reversion is five years and the initial yield is 4%. By reference to the table it can be seen that the internal rate of return on this basis is 6.87%.

Parry's also contains a similar table but reflecting the internal rate of return with projected growth.

Example 9.4

Ascertain the equated yield or internal rate of return with growth on an investment costing £16,400 producing an initial income of £1,000 per annum. The full rental value is estimated at £2,000 per annum and the time to review is five years. Growth is estimated at 5% per annum.

It can be calculated that the initial yield on the above return is 6% (£1,000 divided by £16,400) and that the rental factor is 2 (the estimated full rental value divided by the initial rent). Given these known variables it can be ascertained from the tables that the equated yield or internal rate of return with growth on this investment is 11.42%.

The Advantages and Disadvantages of the Hardcore Method

As has already been stated, the hardcore method is now being used widely in practice. There are advantages and disadvantages in respect of this method. The method has advantages in the sense that it can be used to isolate the increase in rental value on rent review and reversion. It can thus treat this top slice income in a different way. In a volatile market, it can try to estimate the risk of this top slice. It also appears to be applicable in situations where a valuation may be based on turnover rents where there is a base or core rent calculated and to which is added an additional slice based on the actual turnover of the company operating from the property.

On the other hand, its disadvantages are really that it invokes an artificial division of the income. The security of the reversionary income is not divisible; if the tenants default, then they default in the payment of the whole income, not just the top slice. It is also difficult to value using comparables from the market as the comparables would only provide an equivalent yield on the basis of which two unknown quantities, the hardcore yield and the marginal yield, need to be calculated. In using comparable evidence from a conventional term and reversion valuation, there can be great differences in the calculation where the term income is substantially below the current full market rental value. However, where the system was useful in the market of the late 1980s and 1990s was that any downturn in the market could mean a reduction of rental at the next rent review and therefore the ability to layer the income into different slices can mean that the top slice can be treated more appropriately with its inherent risk, possibly being ignored completely in some cases. It could also be used as a valuation method where there are contractual agreements to put the income at review above a market rental value as this will mean that this increase at review is again very risky because it makes a tenant uncompetitive and reluctant to pay the rent.

Criticisms of overvaluation of the core income in the hardcore method and undervaluation of the marginal income really arise because of the uses of an inappropriate schedule of discount rates based on conventional term and reversion yield rather than direct comparables. The high risk of the top slice rental relative to the hardcore rent needs to be taken into account.

The Treatment of Fixed Increases

Properties where the lease terms provide for predetermined fixed increases in rent are not true reversionary investments. This is because generally the initial rent represents the full rack-rent. The increases provided for in the lease generally reflect both sides' views about the likely change in rental levels, although for various reasons including bargaining power this may not be the case. It is suggested that the prime valuation approach to this type of problem should be to capitalise each tranche of income at a fixed interest rate. Where the increases are due to take place say every five years and appear to reflect a reasonable anticipation of growth, then a secondary method of valuation might be to capitalise only the initial income either in perpetuity where freehold or for the period of the lease where leasehold at an appropriate low all-risks yield. Example 9.5 illustrates the recommended procedure.

Example 9.5

Value a freehold interest let for 99 years at an initial net rent of £1,000 per annum rising to £2,000 per annum after 33 years, and £3,000 per annum after 66 years. Assume an appropriate fixed interest rate of 12%.

First 33 years				
Income		pa	£1,000	
YP 33 years @ 12%			8.14	£8,140
Next 33 years				
Income		pa	£2,000	
YP 33 years @ 12%	8.14			
PV £1 in 33 years @ 12%	0.0238			
			1.194	£388
Last 33 years				
Income		pa	£3,000	
YP perp. @ 12%	8.33			
PV £1 in 66 years @ 12%	0.00056		0.0047	£14
				£8,542

Notes
(i) The procedure is to capitalise each level of income for the period over which it is received, and to defer it for the period which elapses before it begins to be received.
(ii) The income for the last 33 years is capitalised in perpetuity. This conventional practice is adopted because the difference between capitalising in perpetuity and capitalising for 33 years when the period of deferment is as long as 66 years is negligible.

(iii) In this instance the initial yield is 11.7% which is only fractionally below the capitalisation rates adopted throughout, and therefore to have valued the initial income in perpetuity at 12% or thereabouts would not have produced a significantly different answer to that produced by the fuller method adopted above.

Leaseholds

Rising (or falling) profit rents may arise for a variety of reasons. They may be valued by either the *term and reversion* method or the *hardcore* method. However, if a dual rate basis is adopted with such calculations, a conventional approach will produce an inaccurate result in so far as the replacement of capital is concerned. This is because by notionally dividing the investment income into tranches or layers an implication is made that each will require the provision of a separate sinking fund to recoup it. The amount left in the fund from the 'term' sinking fund will continue to grow during the reversion and there will be an over-replacement of capital. In practice, all that is required is a single sinking fund for the life of the investment to recoup the whole capital outlay. This would be a traditional approach to sinking fund investment. Various more mathematically correct methods have been propounded including the annual equivalent method, the double sinking fund method[5] and the sinking fund method.[6] There is also an approximate method worked out by P.W. Pannell which is far quicker and probably sufficiently accurate for most purposes. Not all these approaches are considered here, but consideration is given to the double sinking fund and Pannell methods.

The *double sinking fund* method makes use of the fact that the error in the traditional two-stage approach does not occur if single rate tables are used. The method involves taking out a sinking fund over the full life of the investment on the overall capital value which cannot of course be known until the valuation is completed and therefore requires the use of algebra, the capital value being denoted as 'P'. The annual sinking fund instalment is then deducted from the overall income, leaving only spendable income, which may be capitalised using single rate tables. This is carried out for both stages and the results are added together. It will be evident, however, that the capital will have been replaced twice, once at the accumulative rate and once at the remunerative rate(s). This is because the single rate YP contains a remunerative rate sinking fund. It is not necessary to replace the capital at the remunerative rate(s) and hence the capital value deferred at the remunerative rate(s) is added back to the valuation.

As regards the *Pannell* method, this again makes use of the single rate table but this time in a conventionally laid-out valuation, adjusting to take account of the effect an accumulative rate sinking fund would have, by multiplying the answer by a factor comprising the ratio of the figure of dual rate YP for the whole period to the figure of single rate YP for that period. Where the remunerative rates in the two stages of the valuation differ, an intermediate rate must be adopted at this final stage.

The discrepancies which may arise between the various methods depend partly on whether or not the valuations are carried out on a tax-adjusted basis. Some of the methods are illustrated in the following example. Different rates are used on term and reversion in this example to illustrate some of the theoretical problems involved, although in practice, as has been previously noted, an equivalent yield method may well be used whereby the same rate is adopted throughout.

Example 9.6

An office property is let for a term of nine years at a rent of £10,000 per annum net. The head lessee has sublet it at a rent of £20,000 per annum net on a lease with four years unexpired. The full rental value is £30,000 per annum net. Value the head lessee's interest assuming a remunerative rate for the term of 8% and for the reversion 10%, an accumulative rate of 4% throughout, and a tax rate of 40%.

Conventional Method:

Term

Rent receivable under sublease	net pa	£20,000	
Rent payable under head lease	net pa	£10,000	
Profit rent		£10,000	
YP 4 years @ 8% and 4% (tax 40%)		2.12	£21,200

Reversion

Full rental value		net pa	£30,000	
Rent payable			£10,000	
Profit rent			£20,000	
YP 5 years @ 10% and 4% (tax 40%)	2.45			
PV £1 in 4 years @ 10%	0.68		1.67	£33,320
Capital Value				£54,520

Double sinking fund method:

Term

Profit rent as before		pa	£10,000
Less ASF to replace P in 9 years @ 4%			0.094P
T$_G$ factor @ 40%	1.67		0.157P
Spendable income	£10,000	–	0.157P

YP 4 years @ 8%			3.31	
			———	£33,100 – 0.52p

Reversion
Profit rent as before		pa	£20,000	
Less ASF to replace				
P in 9 years @ 4%				
adjusted for tax at				
40% as above			0.157P	
Spendable income	£20,000	–	0.157P	
YP 5 years @ 10%	3.79			
PV £1 in 4 years @ 10%	0.68		2.58	£51,600 – 0.405P
Plus repayment of the				
capital replaced by the				
single rate SF:				
PV £1 in 4 years @ 8%	0.735			
× PV £1 in 5 years @ 10%	0.621	$0.456 \times P$		0.456P
				———————
				£84,500 – 0.469P

Therefore P	=	£84,700 – 0.469P
P + 0.469P	=	£84,700
P	=	£57,650

Pannell's method:
Term
Profit rent as before		pa	£10,000	
YP 4 years @ 8%			3.31	£33,100

Reversion
Profit rent as before		pa	£20,000	
YP 5 years @ 10%	3.79			
PV 4 years @ 10%	0.68		2.58	£51,600
				———
				£84,700

$$\times \frac{\text{YP 9 years @ 9\% and 4\% (tax 40\%)}}{\text{YP 9 years @ 9\%}} = \frac{4.04}{5.995} = \quad \frac{0.674}{}$$

£57,100

Hardcore method with Pannell's adjustment
Net income		pa	£10,000	
YP 9 years @ 8%			6.2469	£62,469
Uplift (no uplift in head rent)		pa	£10,000	
YP 5 years @ 12%[i]	3.6048			
× PV £1 4 years @ 12%	0.6355		2.2909	£22,909
				———
				£85,378

$$£85,378 \times \frac{\text{YP 9 years @ 9\%[ii] and 4\% (tax 40\%) (4.04)}}{\text{YP 9 years @ 9\% (5.9952)}}$$

$$= \frac{£85,378 \times 4.04}{5.9952}$$

$$= £57,550$$

Notes

(i)   That 12% is about right may be verified by means of the following
       preliminary or check calculation:

'Whole' profit rent	pa	£20,000
YP 9 years @ 10% and 4% (tax 40%)		3.88	£77,600
'Bottom Slice' profit rent	pa	£10,000
YP 9 years @ 8% and 4% (tax 40%)		4.21	£42,100
Capital value of marginal income		£35,500
÷ income		£10,000
YP		3.55

This YP figure represents the YP 9 years @ x% + 4% (tax 40%). From
inspection of the appropriate table it will be seen that the correct
remunerative rate is about 12%.

(ii)   This represents an approximate weighted average yield. There are
       four percentage points between the 8% (hardcore) and 12% (marginal)
       rates. The capitalised hardcore income represents about 75% of the
       total 'valuation' (before application of the Pannell adjustment). Hence
       a weighted average yield would be approximately 9%.

Variations on the above approaches would include use of the
hardcore method but using dual rates throughout and avoiding the
Pannell adjustment. This would not be quite as accurate
mathematically. Also in the hardcore method it is sometimes
argued that the whole rents should be capitalised and then the
head rent capitalised separately at a high fixed interest rate and
deducted from the remainder on a capital basis as discussed in the
previous chapter. The interest rates in use in this particular example
are in any event fairly high and the term fairly short. However, it
may well be appropriate in the case of a long lease subject to a fixed
ground rent but where the occupational rents can be varied. This
would seem to be one way of reflecting the gearing effect of such
investments. Further variations (beyond the scope of the question)
would of course be to value on a non tax-adjusted basis or a
different tax-adjusted basis or with different accumulative rates, or
on DCF or single rate bases. In fact, a single rate or DCF basis
would make all the above complicated calculations unnecessary.

Taxation Aspects

As shown in previous chapters, gross-of-tax and net-of-tax
valuations of constant income flows produce the same results.
Where the income flow varies, however, different results are
produced by the two approaches. A net-of-tax valuation succeeds
in off-setting the advantage to a high rate taxpayer of a
reversionary investment. This would be correct if it could be shown
that the market for this type of investment is prepared to bid up the
price to the point where the tax advantage is completely off-set and

hence the property made comparable with fully income-producing investments. The vendor should no doubt be aware of the likely purchasers for this type of investment and value accordingly, although it is quite possible that the full tax advantage could not be offset, particularly in view of the possible liability to capital gains tax on the gain at a later date.

The following example illustrates the difference between gross and net-of-tax valuations of a reversionary investment. Two alternative net-of-tax bases are shown.

Example 9.7

Value a freehold property let for £1,000 per annum net for five years with a reversion to the full rental value of £2,000 per annum net assuming a gross-of-tax equivalent yield of 10%.

Valuation by Traditional Approach

Term			
Net income	pa	£1,000	
YP 5 years 10%		3.7908	£3,791
Reversion			
FRV	net pa	£2,000	
YP rev to perp. 5 years @ 10%		6.2092	12,418
			£16,209

Net-of-tax basis (assuming income tax @ 45%)

Term			
Income	pa	£1,000	
Less tax @ 45%		450	
Net-of-tax income		£550	
YP 5 years @ 5.50%		4.2703	£2,349
Reversion			
FRV	pa	£2,000	
Less tax @ 45%		900	
Net-of-tax income		£1,100	
YP rev to perp. 5 years @ 5.5%		13,912	£15,302
			£17,651

Possible hardcore net-of-tax basis

Hardcore income	pa	£1,000	
YP perp. @ 10%		10	£10,000
Marginal income	pa	£1,000	
YP perp. @ 10%		10	
× PV £1 5 years @ 10%	0.7651	7.651	£7,651
(tax @ 45%)			
			£17,651

Note
The tax adjusted PVs consist of the PV £1 at the net-of-tax rate. In this example this is 5.5%.

The gross of tax valuation could of course have been carried out on a hardcore basis with similar results. The hardcore net-of-tax basis shown could have been produced by means of a true net-of-tax approach throughout the valuation including the capitalisation of the perpetual income on a net-of-tax basis. This again would not have affected the result. Where it is required to use different rates of interest on term and reversion then a *split reversion* method may be adopted which again can be carried out net-of-tax. The term would be valued in the normal way as would the hardcore element of the reversion. The marginal element of the reversion would need to be valued on a net-of-tax basis.

The Finance Act 1965 introduced a tax on long-term capital gains. (Much of the legislation is updated by the Capital Gains Tax Act 1979 and various Finance Acts.) Such gains are currently taxed at the taxpayer's marginal rate on a gain or that part of the gain which exceeds £5,000 in any one year. The Act provides for deduction of allowable expenditure of a capital nature in computing the gain; it makes provision for part disposals, and, most importantly, it only applies to gains since 1965 – thus the gain made on assets acquired before 1965 and disposed of after 1965 must be apportioned so that that part of the gain which occurred before 1965 is excluded from the calculation. There is now the option to elect for March 31 1982 value in place of cost for assets held on or before that date, thereby restricting taxation to gains after that date. Methods for excluding the pre-1965 gain are provided for in the Act. Acquisition costs and enhancement expenditure can be increased after a year in line with inflation (measured by RPI) on post-1981 gain or part of gain (see Finance Act 1982).

Capital gains resulting from the development potential of land have for many years been regarded as a case for special taxation treatment by some politicians. Under current legislation, however, they are not treated differently from normal capital gains, except where they are relieved as part of a garden of a private house.

As regards taxation of assets passing on death, the old Estate Duty provisions are now replaced by the more comprehensive Inheritance Tax, which also makes general provision for the taxation of life-time transfers. This tax was introduced by the Finance Act 1984, but with provision for potentially exempt transfers which can remove most lifetime transfers from the scope of Inheritance Tax.

With regard to the taxation of premiums, premiums for leases not exceeding 50 years are treated partly as capital and partly as income.

It is possible to take account of capital gains tax in any net-of-tax appraisal. For example, if a valuation or analysis allowing for growth is to be carried out and it is anticipated that the property would be sold in the foreseeable future and that no roll-over relief could be obtained (not generally obtainable for investors), then some specific provision for this future incidence of tax could be made. However, reversionary investments increase in value up to the date of the reversion regardless of any growth in rents or inflation in the economy. Therefore the need to consider capital gains tax in a net-of-tax valuation of such properties is obvious. The problem is that in almost all instances it is not known if and when the property will be sold and therefore what tax if any will be payable and when such payments will become due. Any income tax advantage which arises on a reversionary investment as illustrated in the previous section may be entirely or partly offset by a future capital gains tax liability arising on the increase in value of the reversionary income.

Opinions differ as to the need to make allowance for the effects of taxation in valuing reversionary investments. There is the view that unless the market is known to be influenced by such factors then no tax adjustments should be made in the valuation. There is also the added difficulty of analysing market data to take account of tax factors. Hence the conclusions of the Trott Report that valuations taking account of capital gains tax are impracticable. When carried out on a subjective basis for a particular vendor or purchaser, the taxation implications of a transaction will of course play a significant part in the calculations.

As a footnote, it may be observed that research has also been carried out into the effect of the Enterprise Zone Scheme on industrial rents. This concluded that rent levels inside the Zone were higher than those in the periphery owing to two thirds of the rates exemption benefit going to the landlord in the form of increased rent. A valuation in such a situation might seek to isolate this top slice of the income arising from the rates benefit and value it separately for the period of the benefit only. The underlying true rental value (excluding the Enterprise Zone influence) would on the other hand be valued in perpetuity.[7]

DCF Approaches

The short-cut DCF approach was discussed earlier. The DCF approaches are alternatives to the traditional term and reversion valuation. The DCF approach has been examined in Chapter 7 on rack-rented freeholds; here the approach can be extended by the use of term and reversionary rents for the time periods and a growth rate applied to the reversion.

A distinction has to be made here between the short-cut DCF used earlier and the Real Value/Equated Yield Hybrid which is based on the Real Value approach suggested by Ernest Wood but developed by Baum and Crosby.[8]

The short-cut DCF is:
Term: Rent Passing
× YP 3 years @ e%

Reversion to FRV
× amount of £1 for 3 years @ g%
× YP in perp. @ k%
× PV £1 in 3 years @ e%

where
g% pa   = the implied rental growth per annum
e%   = equated yield
3   = number of years to rent review
k%   = all risks yield of comparable

(The equated yield is used to capitalise the rent passing over the term and also to discount the capital values over this period. This is because the rent passing is fixed and does not reflect market conditions. The full rental value is inflated to the time of the reversion at the implied growth rate and then capitalised at the all-risks yield.) The short-cut DCF thus does not bother with inflating the rent through the reversion period; thus the discount rate for the all-risks yield is used on the reversion.

The *Real Value/Equated Yield Hybrid* suggested by Baum and Crosby involves the calculation of the IRFY (Inflation Risk-Free Yield) which is the real interest rate (the market rate with inflation taken out, sometimes called the initial yield). This approach to the reversionary calculation is the same as the short-cut DCF except that the reversion is not inflated. Values are discounted at the IRFY rather than the equated yield, thus the calculation is:

Term: Rent Passing
× YP 3 years @ e% (same as above)

Reversion to FRV
× YP @ k%
× PV £1 in 3 years @ IRFY

The calculation of IRFY comes from the general calculation of interest rates (see Isaac & Steley,[9] Chapter 4):

$$(1 + e) = (1 + g)(1 + i)$$

where
i% is the initial yield
g% is the growth rate
e% is the equated yield

Here i% is the IRFY

thus
$$i = \frac{(1 + g)}{(1 + e)} - 1$$

To find g, Crosby's calculations use the Implied Rate of Rental Growth formula which is stated as:

$$(1 + g)^t = \frac{\text{YP in perp. @ k\% - YP for t years @ e\%}}{\text{YP in perp. @ k\% } \times \text{ PV £1 for t years @ e\%}}$$

where
g% pa = the implied rental growth per annum
e%   = equated yield
t   = rent review pattern of comparable
k%   = all risks yield of comparable

A calculation using this approach is shown in Chapter 10. It is suggested that using this valuation approach, there may be some under-valuation because the deferment of the reversion is at a yield which reflects that rental values will grow periodically every five years over the reversionary period whereas they actually grow continuously.

Problems of Over-Rented Freeholds

In a falling market there arise cases of overage. Overage means that the rent passing is higher than the rack-rental in the market. This can arise in two particular cases. First, where the rent passing is greater than the rent on a normal rent review because of the absence of rent reviews. Secondly, it can occur because of a fall in rental values since the last rent review. In the year to end of March 1991, the All Property Rental Growth Index fell 2.4%.[10] The problem of falls in rental values has meant that in many cases the rent passing is less than the current open market value and this, as indicated above, is defined as overage or froth. Overage can also occur when the property is let on abnormally long rent reviews, but here the term overage is misleading, as really it is an open market value but on different terms. Therefore, overage is best defined as the excess rent over the open market rental value on a normal rent review pattern of five years. Crosby and Goodchild in their analysis of the problems of over-renting come to the conclusion that valuers must now use explicit growth calculations and cannot use the top slicing approach used in the hardcore method which had become popular in the 1970s. These authors in their research consider the need to adopt a growth explicit cashflow approach for both the market valuation and the subsequent appraisal of worth in over-rented situations.[11] Problems of over-renting have been considered earlier.

References and Notes

1 Jones Lang Wootton/Estates Gazette/South Bank Polytechnic, *The Glossary of Property Terms*, Estates Gazette, 1989.
2 Polytechnic of Central London, New Study Paper following Trott Report, *Net of Tax Valuation for Freeholds and Leaseholds*.
3 Trott, A.J. *Property Valuation Methods Interim Report*, Polytechnic of South Bank/RICS.
4 St. Quintin, *Tables of Rent Adjustment Factors to a 5-year Rent Review Pattern*, 1981.
5 Attributed to A.W. Davidson.
6 Attributed to M. Greaves.
7 Syms, P. 'Valuation of Industrial Investments', 282EG1116.
8 Baum, A. and Crosby, N. *Property Investment Appraisal*, Routledge, London, 1988.
9 Isaac, D. and Steley, T. *Property Valuation Techniques*, Macmillan, London, 1991.
10 Crosby, N. 'Over Rented Freehold Investment Property Valuation', *Journal of Property Valuation and Investment*, Vol. 10, No. 2, Winter 1991/2, pp. 517–524.
11 Crosby, N. and Goodchild, R. 'Reversionary Freeholds: Problems with Over-Renting', *Journal of Property Valuation and Investment*, Vol. 11, No. 1, Autumn 1992, pp. 67–81.

Further Reading

Fraser, W.D. 'YP or DCF? – A Question of Comparables', 272EG492.
Wood, E. 'Tax and freehold investments', 269EG1012.

Chapter Ten

Further Aspects of Inflation and Growth

Adjustment of Rental Value for Differing Review Patterns

Estimation of full rental value implies estimating the rent at which a property would let on a given set of lease terms. One of these terms will be the frequency of any rent reviews. The standard period between rent reviews in the granting of new leases on commercial properties has since the early 1970s been about five years, and this still applies to most medium to large prime investments. There have been variations around this including three years, seven years, or even two years or one year. The mass of market rental evidence in the case of most medium to large commercial property investments, however, relates to leases with five-year rent reviews. Problems arise where it is necessary to estimate rental value for a lease term or period between rent reviews other than that to which the mass of market evidence relates.

The problem becomes particularly acute where valuers are asked to determine a rental value upon a rent review in a relatively long lease granted some time ago with what now appear to be abnormally long rent review periods, for example, a 42-year lease granted in 1959 with a single review after 21 years.

Mathematical Approaches

There are primarily two different situations which may be encountered. One is the balancing of a lease with no reviews, say for 21 years, with a similar length lease incorporating reviews at say, seven-yearly intervals. The other is concerning the balance which is to be struck between a lease with reviews at certain intervals, say a 14-year lease with seven-year rent review, and a lease with different periods between reviews, say a 15-year lease with five-year rent reviews. The methods which are considered below are mathematically correct for both types of situation.

The use of the various methods relies upon an assumption that rental values will grow year by year into the future, as is implied by the current initial yields acceptable on commercial property investments. The effect of this assumption is that the longer the period between reviews, the greater the hardship the landlord will suffer, and conversely, the greater the benefit the tenant will enjoy unless the rent can be adjusted to offset these effects.

Jack Rose has published *Tables of the Constant Rent.*[1]

These tables are based upon the following formula as simplified.

$$K = \frac{A - B}{A - 1} \times \frac{C - 1}{C - D}$$

where

K = the constant rent

A = Amount of £1 @ R% for L years
  where   R = the lessors required return (risk rate),
  and   L = the length in years of the lease being granted

B = Amount of £1 @ G% for L years
  where   G = the anticipated rate of growth (or inflation) per annum

C = Amount of £1 @ R% for Z years,
  where Z= the interval in years between rent reviews which would normally have been agreed between the parties; and

D = Amount of £1 @ G% for Z years.

The *constant rent* is a factor which, when applied to the rent which would be payable for a normal rent review pattern, will produce the required enhanced rent payable on a longer rent review pattern. The rate R is the equated yield rate. L is the length in years of the lease being granted or of the actual review period in the lease under consideration. Rose himself has suggested that the rate should be that appropriate to valuing short leaseholds.

An example based upon the formula, which may also be checked against the figure in the table, is given below.

Example 10.1

Calculate by use of the 'Constant Rent Tables' formula the rent which would be appropriate upon a review which is to last 21

When the anticipated growth rate exactly equals the lessor's required risk rate – in other words, where G equals R, the formula involves a division by zero, and so becomes useless. In these special circumstances an alternative formula for capital K is used as given in the tables.

years. The lessor's required return on capital is 15%, the anticipated growth rate is 8% per annum, and the normal review period in the market is currently five years upon which basis the premises would let for £10,000 per annum.

$$K = \frac{18.8215 - 5.0338}{18.8215 - 1} \times \frac{2.0114 - 1}{2.0114 - 1.4693}$$

$$K = 1.443 \times £10,000 = £14,430 \text{ pa}$$

An alternative solution to the problem would be by means of *Donaldson's Tables*. It will be recalled from Chapter 7 that if three out of four variables are known or can be estimated, then the fourth can be derived from these tables. In this instance the equated yield and growth rate have been estimated and are assumed to be applicable to either the 21-year or the five-year review pattern. The alternative review patterns, ie 21 years and five years are known. The only unknown quantity is the initial yield. The initial yield represents the ratio of rent to capital value. If the capital value is to remain constant, the initial yield and hence the rent must rise to compensate the investor for the longer review pattern. Hence the ratio of the initial yield appropriate to the long review period to the initial yield appropriate to the normal market review period will be the same as the constant rent factor. The following calculation involving the information in Example 10.1 uses *Donaldson's Tables* to this effect.

Initial yield appropriate to 15% equated yield and 8% per annum growth is approximately 8% for a 5-year review period and 11.56% for a 21-year review period.

$$\frac{11.56}{8} = 1.445$$

As an alternative to using *Donaldson's Tables*, the initial yield in each case may be calculated from the formula given below.

$$I = E - E \left[\frac{(1 + G)^n - 1}{(1 + E)^n - 1} \right]$$

where
E = equated yield
G = growth rate
n = rent review period
I = initial yield

Graphs have been produced showing the normal rental value in relationship to the rental value appropriate to a longer review period, calculated according to these principles. In one case these are shown in the form of rent ratios,[2] and in the other case[3] in the form of percentage increase over the FRV applicable to five-year reviews.

Yet a further solution to this problem may be obtained by the use of *Bowcock's Valuation Tables*. This involves converting the rent obtainable on a normal review pattern lease to the rent obtainable on an annually reviewable basis, which will be initially lower. This figure is termed the *Rental Equivalent on an Annual Tenancy* (REAT). This Rental Equivalent is then converted to an equivalent rental with the longer, actual review pattern *Rental Equivalent on Lease* (REL).

It should be borne in mind that it is not only the effect on the landlord but also the effect on the tenant that should be considered. Even if the dual rate concept is abandoned, it would be appropriate to consider the effects of the taxation of profit rents when considering matters from the tenant's viewpoint.

Rental Adjustments in Practice

In practice, tenants tend to look short-term and landlords long-term, and therefore there is a conflict which cannot necessarily be resolved by mathematics. The best answer to the problem posed in Example 10.1 would be to ascertain what rent would be obtained in the market by offering such a lease without reviews. It would appear that landlords are not inclined to test the market in this way, and there is therefore unlikely to be any suitable current market evidence. Landlords almost invariably prefer frequent in-built rent reviews. It is becoming recognised that the answers produced by the type of mathematical exercise carried out above are likely to be higher than those which would be bid by tenants in the market in practice. The majority of agreements will be given different interpretations by either party and in the case of three-, five- or seven-year rent reviews, the differences in rent, even if calculated on a mathematical basis as above, are so slim as to be capable of different interpretations. In practice there may be no variation in rent between a five-year and a rent review pattern on a seven-year basis. Other valuers consider that a 5% 'spot' addition might be appropriate in such cases, or a 2% for each year over the fifth. It probably depends on the type of property in question as some properties are still let on the basis of seven-year reviews whereas some are let on the basis of three-year reviews, or even less. Most valuers find it difficult to agree a specific addition in such cases. There is no doubt, however, that agreements are being reached for a significant 'uplift' in the case of 14-year or 21-year reviews. Cases have been recorded of 20% uplift for a 14-year review and landlords seeking a 30% uplift for 21-year reviews. It would appear that these figures are probably higher than average however, and a more normal uplift for a 10 to 14 year cycle might be 10%. Other 'rules of thumb' are for the uplift as calculated by the mathematical methods set out above, to be reduced by possibly as much as a half or two-thirds to adequately reflect the tenant's viewpoint in the calculations.

Commentary

The following are arguments against the Constant Rent (or *Equated Rent* or *Premium Rent*) principle.

(i)   In the case of lease renewals or negotiations for a new lease, then an 'uplift', however calculated, is undoubtedly appropriate if an abnormally long review period is freely negotiated. In the case of a rent review, however, the terms of the existing lease were freely negotiated at the outset and the presumption could be made that both parties reflected the risk of higher rates of future inflation in the terms which they agreed initially, and did not anticipate that there would be a re-calculation in the landlord's favour upon a review. In any event, if the landlord only recently purchased the property at a relatively high yield which reflected the nature of the lease, then he would be doubly compensated for any disadvantage by obtaining an enhanced rent on review.

(ii) The growth rate to be used is speculative.

(iii) It is unlikely that tenant traders will be willing to speculate the profit represented by the current revenue against the uncertainty of a notional future profit rent. Such notional future profit rent would be created by the fact that the constant rent represents a 'front loaded' risk to the tenant. In other words, he will be paying over the normal market rent at the beginning of the lease in return for paying under the normal market rent towards the end of the lease. A tenant may encounter problems in assigning a lease at a rent negotiated in accordance with constant rent principles.

The following arguments are in favour of the constant rent principle.

(a)   The counter-argument to argument (i) above is that, whether or not there is reason in this argument, the terms of the rent review clause and any current market evidence of longer rent review patterns would prevail. It is the sparsity of such evidence, however, which creates the problem. The benefit to the tenant is such that he may pay a higher rent.

(b)   The counter-argument to argument (ii) above is that both land-lord and tenant are speculating about the future rate of growth. If it is lower than that predicted then the tenant will be the loser, if it is higher than that predicted then the landlord loses.

(c)   The trader tenant is able to protect himself against inflation by increasing the price of his goods and services and therefore it is not reasonable that he should be able to benefit at the landlord's expense.

As an alternative to being faced with the problem of a long rent review cycle, a landlord in practice may well be prepared to pay a substantial premium to his tenant for the surrender of his lease in return for the grant of a new lease on modern lease terms. Marriage value is released in such a procedure and this may be shared between the parties. *Marriage value* is the latent value which is released upon the merging of two interests. This may be either a legal merger, as in the case of marrying a freehold and leasehold interest, by the surrender of the lease or the acquisition of the freehold by the lessee, or alternatively a physical merger as in the case of the acquisition of an adjoining property, for example, to make a development scheme more viable. This marriage value is usually split between the parties to the agreement on a basis to be agreed, say 50:50, or in proportion to the value of their respective interests before marriage is taken into account. The effects of taxation on the parties to the agreement should be taken into account in making the necessary calculations.

As an aside, it was held by the Court of Appeal in *National Westminster Bank Ltd* v *BSC Footwear Ltd* ([1981] 1 EGLR 89), to be beyond the powers of the arbitrator to build in more frequent rent reviews upon a rent review where there was, under the terms of the lease, a long period between the review and the expiry, without any intermediate reviews. It was said that 'what the landlord's predecessors in title gave away these landlords cannot now take back'. It should be emphasised, however, that there was no reference in this case to the Constant Rent Principle.

The Effect on Capital Value of Differing Review Patterns

In strict mathematical terms, a lengthening of the rent review cycle, with a consequent increase in rental value, will not affect capital value as there will be a corresponding increase in the initial yield and hence reduction in years' purchase. The following calculations show this to be the case using the information provided in Example 10.1, that is, a rental valuation to be carried out on the basis of a 21-year period to next review, an equated yield of 15%, an anticipated growth rate of 8% per annum, and a normal market review pattern of five years producing a rental value of £10,000 per annum. In this case, rather than using *Donaldson's Tables*, the initial yields are calculated precisely, using the formula given on page 159, so that the two capital values are shown to be identical.

The rental values appropriate to both situations have already been calculated or derived from the appropriate table. It is then necessary to calculate the implied initial yield, using the data given in the question, for both situations. This initial yield then performs its function as a capitalisation rate, and the capital values are then shown to be the same in both cases, which is, of course, the principle upon which the Constant Rent Tables are based.

Valuation for 5-Year Review Cycle

$$I = 0.15 - 0.15 \ \frac{1.08^5 - 1}{1.15^5 - 1}$$

$$0.15 - 0.15 \ \frac{0.4693}{1.01136}$$

$$I = \underline{0.0804}$$

Rental Value with 5-year reviews	£10,000 pa
YP perp. @ 8.04%	12.438
Capital value	£124,380

Valuation for 21-Year Lease (No Review) or 21 Years to Next Review

$$I = 0.15 - 0.15 \ \frac{1.08^{21} - 1}{1.15^{21} - 1}$$

$$= \underline{0.116015}$$

Rental value with 21 year reviews	£14,430
YP perp. @ 11.6%	8.6195
Capital value	£124,380

In practice, investments with short rent review cycles are likely to sell for more than investments with long rent review cycles, other things being equal, because of possible disagreements with tenants over the application of the constant rent principle and the inherent risks in long review periods.

These principles involving the interaction of rent and yield have more general application. For example, good potential tenants such as government departments, are frequently able to negotiate lower rents than other potential tenants because owners know that such lettings create good investments with correspondingly low yields (high years' purchases) resulting in capital value being unaffected. The converse may apply – a bad potential tenant may have to pay a relatively high rent to offset the reduction in the years' purchase which a subsequent purchaser of the investment applies in his valuation. Here again though, the 'cancelling out' process may not always apply because the factors which determine yield and which determine rent are, to some extent, different, reflecting the different priorities of investors and tenants.

The Treatment of Future Outgoings and Liabilities

With regard to the treatment of future outgoings and liabilities in valuation, the traditional approach is to incorporate them into the valuation at their current cost and discount them at either the remunerative rate or at a sinking fund accumulative rate. Annual outgoings are implicitly discounted at the remunerative rate by being deducted from income, the net income then being capitalised at this rate. In the case of unavoidable future capital liabilities (as opposed to future optional expenditure), many valuers were once in favour of discounting at the low sinking fund rate.

The use of the remunerative rate throughout in this context is logical so long as it is considered that future changes in the cost of liabilities and outgoings will move in line with changes in rental income, as these different items are not treated separately by the conventional method. A DCF example will make this explicit.

Example 10.2

Value a freehold property, currently let at a net rack rental income of £1,000 per annum. The lease incorporates rent reviews at five-yearly intervals. In order to maintain the income, it will be necessary to spend £5,000 (at current costs) on refurbishment after five years. Assume an equated yield of 15% and a growth rate of 8%.

Valuation by DCF

Years (inc.)	Cash flow at today's prices	Amt. £1 @ 8%	Projec- ted cash flow	YP 5 yrs @ 15%	PV £1 @ 15%	YP perp. @ 8%[(iii)] × PV £1 @ 15%	Present value
1st–5th	£1,000	N/A	£1,000	3.3522			£3,352
6th		1.4693[(ii)]	£1,469		0.4323		£635
8th	£1,000	1.4693	£1,469		0.3759		£552
9th	£1,000	1.4693	£1,469		0.3269		£480
10th	£1,000	1.4693	£1,469		0.2843		£418
11th– perp.	£1,000	2.1589	£2,159			3.09	£6,671
							£9,186

Notes
(i)   This is the expenditure of £5,000 less the year's income of £1,000.

(ii) This multiplier remains constant for years 6 to 10 as the rent cannot change over this period.
(iii) Future growth is not reflected in the cash flows after year 10 and hence the implied initial yield rate is adopted to capitalise them in perpetuity. The figure of 8% was derived from *Donaldson's Tables*.

Conventional Valuation using the Derived Initial Yield

Rent reserved	net pa	£1,000
YP perp. @ 8%		12.5
		£12,500
Less future expenditure	£5,000	
× PV £1 5 years @ 8%	0.6801	£3,400
		£9,100

Note
The discrepancy arising between this answer and that in the first calculation arises due to approximations used in the calculations.

The use of the sinking fund accumulative rate is a more cautious approach.

As regards the treatment of annual outgoings during an inflationary period, it may be that annual outgoings rise while income remains fixed between any reviews. It is clearly, therefore, important, to estimate outgoings taking account of inflation. This could possibly be carried out on a DCF basis.

If a true sinking fund approach is adopted to future outgoings and liabilities, such as the need to rebuild or refurbish the whole or parts of an income-producing property in the future, then it is the true estimated future costs of the works which must be saved for. As the escalation in costs is likely to outstrip any net of tax income which could be earned in a sinking fund investment, unrealistic sums would need to be set aside each year to provide for this eventuality, thereby reducing – and possibly drastically reducing – the remunerative yield on the investment. Once again, therefore, inflation throws into doubt the whole concept of a sinking fund. Some way will have to be found to meet the expenditure as and when it arises, out of income or borrowing at that time. To this extent, the solution promulgated above in Example 10.2, is only correct if the deficit in the sixth year could be met from income from other investments or by borrowing at the equated yield rate of 15%. Alternatively, the matter could be dealt with by setting aside the sum of £2,999 (being the present value of that future deficit) and investing this at 15% per annum to meet the anticipated deficiency in that year. This assumes that the investor pays no income tax on that 15% per annum return, or otherwise the analysis would need to be carried out on a net of tax basis.

Over-Rented Freehold Properties

Over-renting occurs in a period of falling rents – for instance where properties are let at rents which are above the rents which could be achieved in the open market. The difference in the amount of rent passing and the current open market rental is termed overage or froth. Overage is also sometimes referred to when a property is let on an abnormally long review pattern but strictly this could be considered the open market value on different terms.

Thus overage can be defined as the excess of rent over open market value based on a normal review pattern of five years.

Overage Related to Abnormal Review Patterns

Crosby and Goodchild[4] suggest five approaches to dealing with this:

- Ignore and value at the full rental value.
- Ignore overage as an addition, value the full rental and add the overage, this is then valued to rent review at a higher yield.
- Include overage as an addition as previously mentioned, but adjust the all risks yield on the core income at a higher yield.
- Value as a conventional term and reversion, valuing the term at a higher yield with a reversion at the rack rent.
- Use a short-cut growth explicit DCF (see later example).

Crosby and Goodchild suggest that conventional approaches may overvalue the term and undervalue the reversion. In the short-term growth explicit DCF, the valuation allows the fixed term to be specifically dealt with.

Overage Caused by Rental Value Reduction

In this case, the additional income is a bonus until the next rent review and the issue is how this is to be treated. The use of a conventional and a growth explicit calculation are given below as suggested by Crosby and Goodchild.

Example

A property has a yield at a rack rent of 5%. It was let one year ago at a rental of £150,000 and thus has four years unexpired. The full rental value at present is £100,000 per annum.

A conventional approach would value the core income and overage separately.

Traditional/hardcore approach
Core income:

Full rental value	£100,000	
YP perp @ 5%[1]		20.00
		£2,000,000

Overage:

Passing rent	£150,000	
Less Full Rental Value	£100,000	
	£50,000	
YP 4 years @ 14%[2]	2.9137	
		£145,685
Capital value		£2,145,685

Notes
1. The initial yield (i) used on the core income is 5%.
2. The return on the overage is assessed as 14%.

The debate on the use of this valuation relates to the security of the core income and the overage and how the reduction of this overage should be treated on the assumption that rents may grow until the overage is eliminated at a subsequent review.

In a growth explicit DCF calculation the equated yield of 12% or target yield is assumed. The growth rate will need to be calculated using:

$$(1 + g)^t = \frac{\text{YP in perp. @ k\% − YP for t years @ e\%}}{\text{YP in perp. @ k\% × PV £1 for t years @ e\%}}$$

where
g% pa = the implied rental growth per annum
e% = equated yield
t = rent review pattern of comparable
k% = all risks yield of comparable

(This is a variation on the growth equation shown in the previous chapter.)

Here the growth rate calculation gives the growth rate (g%) as 7.64%.

where
e% = 12%
t = 5 years
k% = 5%

Growth explicit approach

Term: Rent passing	£150,000	
YP 4 years @ 12%[1]	3.0373	
		£455,595
Reversion to Full Rental Value	£100,000	
Amt of £1 in 4 years @ 7.64%[2]	1.3422	
		£134,220

YP in perp. @ 5%[3]   20.0000
× PV £1 in 4 years @ 12%[4]   0.6355
                                                    12.7104
                                                              £1,705,936
                                                              £2,161,531

Notes
1. Based on a target equated yield of 12% but may be varied intuitively; may be higher to accord with the hardcore valuation as set out earlier.
2. Growth rate as calculated.
3. All risks yield.
4. Equated yield.

The use of DCF techniques in the form of a short-cut or modified DCF is being adopted by the profession to deal with over-renting and thus knowledge of the application of the techniques is vital.

References and Notes

1 Rose, J.J. *Tables of the Constant Rent*, The Technical Press, Oxford.
2 Clark, R. *Rent Ratio Graph.*
3 Warren, B.R. *Rent Review Analysis Graphs.*
4 Crosby, N. and Goodchild, R. 'Problems with over-renting', *Journal of Property Valuation and Investment*, Vol. 11, No. 1, 1992, pp. 67–81.

Further Reading

College of Estate Management, (various) Property Valuation handbooks.
Darlow, C. 'Indexing Valuations', 263EG327.
Sykes, S. 'Valuation Models: action or reaction', 267EG1108.
Sykes, S. 'Refurbishment and Future Rental Growth: The Applications', 272EG1231.

PART III

INVESTMENT APPRAISAL

Chapter Eleven

Investment Risk

Individual Risk

Risk is a major determinant of return. Modern Portfolio Theory sees the investment decision as a trade-off between risk and expected return. Much research in property risk has been devoted to the application of measures already devised for equity investment in the property market and these are related to portfolio risk analysis. Waldy[1] suggests that the main argument for considering single asset risk to be equally as important as portfolio risk is that in practice, most investors in the UK are not able to diversify away the individual property element of risk adequately. Waldy suggests that there is a hierarchy of approaches in considering single asset risk, starting with the intuitive approach used in traditional valuation for the assessment of the all risks yield (ARY), which is assessed in accordance with the risk profile of the property. The ARY is thus an implicit assessment that is open to criticisms of subjectivity. Explicit approaches are used in discounted cash flow appraisals, including sensitivity analysis and scenario testing. Sensitivity analysis measures the effect upon capital value by a change in variable inputs in the calculation. Scenario testing postulates various situations by assigning appropriate values to the variables to test for different scenario effects. Risk-adjusted discount rates can be used to provide for a premium to reflect risk. Certainty equivalent techniques, through probability and the removal of downside risk, calculate risk-free cash flows that can be capitalised using the risk-free rate of return. Probability analysis is inherent in these calculations. The problems associated with this area of risk analysis include the continuous distribution of variables, skewness of samples and serial correlation between cash flows.

Lack of certainty regarding the expected return results in the devaluation of the return. Sources of risk in a property investment decision may arise from: tenant risk; sector risk; structural risk;

legislation risk; taxation risk; planning risk and legal risk.[2] Morley[3] suggests the following aspects of risk in property investment: rental value and rental growth; yield on sale and timing of sale; age and obsolescence; lease structure; liquidity; management costs; taxation and inflation. He also cites the fact that risk analysis is a major factor in affecting property investment projects.

Finance theory suggests three broad categories of risk: business, financial and liquidity. Business risk is due to the uncertainty of future income flows, based on the nature of the firm's business. Financial risk arises from the method of financing an investment. Liquidity risk is introduced by the availability/access to the secondary market for an investment. Another way of analysing risk is to look at the effect of risk on money income and real income. This depends on whether the investment is inflation-proof or inflation-prone, thus this analysis looks at the risk of inflation affecting cashflows. Money risk is the risk of variation in monetary income flows. Real risk is the risk of variation in real income flows (ie excluding inflation). Examples of real and monetary risks are shown in Table 11.1.

Table 11.1 Real and monetary risks

Level of risk	Real risk	Monetary risk
Low	Index-linked gilts	Fixed interest gilts
	Equities	Bank deposits
	Property	Index-linked gilts
	Bank deposits	Property equities
High	Fixed interest gilts	

Source: Baum and Crosby[2]

Risk can attach to a single property or a portfolio of property or investments. Markowitz[4] developed a basic portfolio model that suggested that risk could be reduced within a portfolio by combining assets whose returns demonstrated less than perfect positive correlation (ie a spread of risk). Property as an investment is prone to both unsystematic and systematic risks. Unsystematic or specific risk relates to individual investment and by diversifying, this is reduced in the portfolio. Systematic risk is related to the market and cannot be diversified away. The market risk is quantified as β (beta) and this measures the sensitivity of income movements of the portfolio relative to movements in the market. A β of 1.5 would mean that if rents in the sector fell 1%, the rental level of the portfolio would fall 1.5%. Thus the effect of a balanced portfolio is to reduce, but not remove, property investment risk.

The rational investor seeks to maximise return but often return is not the only criterion. Factors such as capital and income growth can be incorporated into the calculation by the use of DCF techniques, but other factors such as liquidity and ease of management present more difficulty and these are dealt with by intuitive policy decisions. Risk analysis is a standard management technique and is a useful application to enable the analysis, used in property investment, to equate with those used in other investment media. These techniques are required, along with increased knowledge of statistical techniques and the use of computers to enable the analysis to facilitate the analysis. The definition of risk is defined in many ways, but, for a property investment, it is the level of probability that a required return, measured in terms of capital value and income, will be achieved. Over time, the variance of actual return compared to expected return (the volatility) could be measured and used to help determine probability levels. Risk is about the probability of receipt of future returns; this can have a number of possible results and the chances that any particular outcome will result will vary. The degree to which actual performance may exceed the expected performance is called the upside potential, while the amount by which it falls below expectation is the downside risk. It is with the latter concept that investors are most concerned, particularly with an investment funded by borrowed money. Upside potential is regarded as the 'added bonus' over and above the targeted return. The distinction between risk and uncertainty is that risk is concerned with variances and probabilities, with variations in return usually calculated in terms of standard deviations, a measure of the dispersion of return around the mean. The term *standard deviation* can be explained in terms of the greater the standard deviation, the more widely the returns are spread from the expected return and the greater the risk and vice versa. Uncertainty is different in dust no probability can be ascribed to the probable outcome, the assessment must remain qualitative not quantitative although investors may feel fit to deal with such situations by the use of mini-max criteria or by using a payback technique.

To summarise, risk evaluation aids the decision-making process and helps the investor answer the following questions:

(i) What is the expected rate of return or the most likely outcome?

(ii) What is the probability of making a loss as measured against a target return cost of borrowing or alternative investment return? Alternatively, what is the probability of exceeding the target?

(iii) What is the variability or spread of returns in relation to the expected return? (Low volatility (risk) is traded off against return.)

Types of Risk

The types of risk that may be encountered by an investor are summarised in the following paragraphs and are related to the income flow, future outgoings, capital value and market value.

Income Flow

Any investment other than a government stock carries the risk of default. With equities, the size or frequency of the dividend is not secure. With property, the risk of default on an investment will depend on the strength of the covenant and, in the case of reversionary property, risk is attached to the projected income flow, voids and size. With leasehold properties, there are problems of dilapidation claims. Many appraisals of property, especially in the boom years of the 1980s, had built in explicit expectation of rental growth, with the amount depending on the age and type of properly and projected demand. Growth can be built into the capitalisation rate; a lower rate means more risk because of risk that the growth rate will not be achieved. Risk of not achieving target returns is greater with low-yielding property.

Future Outgoings

Risk is very relevant to direct property investment. Even with a new unit let on full repairing and insuring (FRI) terms, there is a strong possibility that technology and fashion change can affect a property sufficiently so that premature obsolescence can set in. This will mean a large future expense not reflected in the original appraisal. Any property at risk from obsolescence will need to build in estimates of future refurbishment in the initial investment appraisal. Other unexpected outgoings could be: structural failures due to inherent defects, unforeseen legal costs or government legislation such as the Counter Inflation Act 1973, which led to a rent freeze.

Capital Value

Capital value depends on the expected income flow. This reflects the level of likely outgoings but even without the variations, the capital value can vary with the yield. Capital value predictions may prove inaccurate because of general imperfections in market knowledge, lack of comparable transactions and the secrecy surrounding deals. There may also be valuation errors; the difference in valuation can affect the return significantly with an error of ± 10%. The fact that values are not tested in the market with the frequency that gilt or equity transactions take place leads to uncertainty regarding capital value.

Market Value

The valuation is normally carried out to open market value (OMV) defined by the *Statement of Asset Valuation Practice and Guidance Notes* provided by the RICS,[5] now superseded by the new 'Red Book'.[6] Frequently, however, the price that the investment actually realises is very different, due to the strength of the market at the moment of sale or due to the presence of the special purchaser. The pressure in some institutions to realise their assets means that the price may be less than the value ascribed. Other risks may be associated with legislation obsolescence, inflation, legal risk, and timing risk. Timing risk is critical to obtain the optimum return. In an uncharted situation, like an adventurous, complex, out-of-town shopping development in the process of construction the final rental value could be hard to predict and the appropriate capitalisation rate yet more difficult. Another risk is holding period; the longer the project life, the greater the uncertainty attached to the likely income flows.

Techniques used to Manage Risk in the Individual Asset

The approaches used to manage risk in the individual asset include payback, expected net present value (ENPV), normal distribution theory, simulation, sensitivity analysis and risk adjustment techniques, certainty equivalent and sliced income approaches. These approaches are not covered in detail in this book and you are also referred to Isaac's book, *Property Investment*.[7] The assessment of risk in practice is limited: Waldy examined risk perception by practitioners and found they envisaged risk in terms of individual sources such as voids or depreciation rather than in investment terms. The results indicated that investors appeared more concerned about single asset risk than portfolio risk and about 90% of the respondents to his survey did not measure risk at all. Those that measured risk used scenarios, sensitivity analysis and probability. Waldy concluded that it would seem prudent for investors to undertake far more analysis and by making greater use of DCF techniques, such as sensitivity analysis, to seek to improve their intuitive 'feel'. For the near future, he concluded, they could follow Hargitay[8] who considered scenarios to be a reasonable interim approach to incorporating risk into property appraisal, pending the resolution of the problems attached to complex probabilistic models.

The Theory of Risk

Risk can be defined in many ways but, for a property investment, it is the level of probability that a required return (measured in terms of capital value and income) will be achieved. Over time, the variance of actual return from expected return (the volatility) could be measured and used to help determine probability levels. Risk is about the estimation of future returns and there can be a number of possible results. The chances that any particular outcome will result will vary according to the risk. In a world where the future is uncertain, decision making involves taking a risk. Investments offer the expectation of high returns from the investor as a reward or compensation for taking the risk involved. So, in this case the perfect capital market does not just display a single interest rate but a continuum of interest rates to reflect the levels of risk. The problems associated with this market are the calculation of the risk (which is associated with any investment), and how the capital markets will price this risk in terms of the interest rates charged.

References

1 Waldy, E.B.D. 'Single asset risk', in P. Venmore-Rowland, P. Brandon and T. Mole (eds.) *Investment, Procurement and Performance in Construction*, RICS, London, 1991.
2 Baum, A. and Crosby, N. *Property Investment Appraisal*, Routledge, London, 1995.
3 Morley, S.J.E. 'The Analysis of Risk in the Appraisal of Property Investments', in A.R. MacLeary and N. Nanthakumaran (eds.) *Property Investment Theory*, E & FN Spon, London, 1988.
4 Markowitz, H. 'Portfolio selection', *Journal of Finance*, Vol. VII, No. 1, March 1952, pp. 79–91.
5 Royal Institution of Chartered Surveyors, *Statement of Asset Valuation Practice and Guidance Notes*, RICS, London, 1992.
6 Royal Institution of Chartered Surveyors, *RICS Appraisal and Valuation Manual*, RICS, London, 1995.
7 Isaac, D. *Property Investment*, Macmillan, London, 1998.
8 Hargitay, S.E. *A Systematic Approach to the Analysis of the Property Portfolio*, Unpublished PhD thesis, University of Reading (quoted in Waldy[1]), 1983.

Chapter Twelve

Computer and Statistical Aids

Computers

All valuers are familiar with the need for efficient means of storing and gaining access to data, together with the need for efficient aids to calculation in the form of valuation tables or electronic calculators. The computer combines both these functions together with other aids to the professions of the land. The computer is a sophisticated and very fast calculating machine with an ability to record information and present it on demand neatly and rapidly and in all kinds of arrays. It cannot make independent judgments but can only carry out instructions. A computer would be an aid to many of the calculations and methods adopted in this book.

The three principle components of any computer system are the machinery (hardware), the operating instructions and system (software) and maintenance for them both (support).

Kirkwood[1] analyses the computer into four main areas. The first of these is described as the 'systems level' which is concerned with the input, output, processing and storage facilities of the computer. The next area concerns the Central Processing Unit and may be described as the 'programming level'. Then there is the 'logic design level' which consists of the logic supporting the computer's operations. Lastly there is the 'Electronic Circuit Design Level'. The surveyor using computers needs to know the first of these areas in order to use the computer properly, preferably the second of these areas as he may wish to write his own programs, and an understanding of the third and fourth areas would provide useful background to his work but would not be essential.

In addition to the computer itself, there are the printers and visual display units. The quality of the printed product is important.

As regards *software*, all instructions to the computer are coded and hence the need for the skilled computer programmer familiar with the language of the particular computer he is operating. A specialist programmer with the statistical and mathematical knowledge associated with valuations in this particular context is also required. Programs can be bought off-the-peg, written individually, or a combination of the two. The reason that more and more valuation models are being written in formulae is that this is the way that they would be entered onto the computer. Programs bought off the peg might be general purpose packages, eg for word processing, or specialist packages, eg for valuations.

The *supporting facilities* are also essential. Normally the machinery should operate smoothly but when things do go wrong it is essential to have skilled assistance available.

The following are among the uses of the computer of which the profession could take advantage:

(i)   Management accounts, including rent review reminders.
(ii)   Matching the requirements of prospective landlords and tenants.
(iii)   Matching the requirements of prospective vendors and investors/purchasers.
(iv)   Providing a statistical background for investment decisions, including information relating to patterns of income and credit and trends in value, and risk analysis (portfolio analysis).
(v)   Development planning and management.
(vi)   Project cost control.
(vii)   Statistical analysis.
(viii) Network analysis.
(ix)   Computer aided design.
(x)   Wordprocessing.

More particularly, the applications of software in valuation may be analysed as follows:

(i)   Yield Analysis.
(ii)   Cash Flow Analysis.
(iii)   Analysis and Forecasting.
(iv)   Risk Analysis and Appraisal/Residual.
(v)   The storage and retrieval of information for comparative assessment, including sales and management details of income and expenditure on properties.
(vi)   Everyday valuations.
(vii)   Investment property valuation.

Spreadsheets

Some of these functions will be appropriate for *spreadsheets*.

This comes within the software category of 'off-the-shelf stand-alone' packages, as opposed to 'off-the-shelf application-specific' packages. The latter are a type of package produced by a software house with a specific market and task in mind. Stand-alone packages such as spreadsheets are more flexible in their use because they can be customised by a user to carry out a wide range of tasks. A spreadsheet is a large ledger sheet. The screen operates as a window to focus on a particular part of the ledger. This type of package has extensive use in valuation. There are in fact some limitations to the spreadsheet valuation packages as against bespoke valuation programs, the latter being more user-friendly than the spreadsheet.

The *database* will enable the valuer to store and retrieve figures for income, operating expenses, capitalisation rates, for use in his valuations and analyses. In the valuation process the valuer will nonetheless still be required to interpret the information thereby provided.

An advanced programmable calculator, with a printer, which fulfils many of the functions of a computer may be an economic way of dealing with some of the problems met with in the valuation profession. These enable greater flexibility than printed tables with greater options of tax and frequency of rent payments, the possibilities of discounted cash flow calculations involving term and reversion problems with uneven rent review patterns, gearing elements and possible future dilapidation claims growth and income and capital taxation aspects.

Programmable calculators are already used by many of the large firms of valuers for DCF type calculations. It is quite likely that in due course computers or programmable calculators will supercede valuation tables due to their ability to calculate quickly a precise YP for example. At present, computers are largely used as a labour-saving device in carrying out calculations which could be done manually. In due course it is likely that surveyors will start to use computers for more adventurous purposes such as systems analysis and risk analysis.

In addition to databases to provide the evidence and analysis for valuation and property transactions, the spreadsheet is also a critical tool to be used by a valuation surveyors in calculations.

The spreadsheet was introduced generally at the beginning of the 1980s. The spreadsheet consists of a computer program which displays on the computer screen a number of cells. Each cell is given a location rather like a map reference and these co-ordinates provide an address in which to put input data and a means by which the relationship between each of the cells can be described. By knowing the addresses of the various cells, by installing data within the cells and by instructing the computer in a relationship between the cells, it is possible to build up a complex calculation across a number of cells and obtain an answer to the calculation. The power of the spreadsheet is its ability to recalculate instantly when one or a number of the inputs into the cells are changed. The investment calculation can thus be changed to allow access of a number of 'what if' scenarios. It may also be used with the input of very simple data to ensure that the calculation process that has been put into the spreadsheet is correct before elaborate calculation. The use of the spreadsheet comes into its own when considering developments in valuation methods, particularly when dealing with discounted cashflow calculations and attempting to apply growth rates to variables or risk probabilities as discussed earlier.

The development of the spreadsheet came mainly in the area of accounting, where it can be seen that the tool was very powerful in managing the complex financial transactions as contained in the accounts of companies and being able to give solutions for the final accounts.

Multiple Regression Analysis

The most simple type of regression analysis enables the analyst to predict the value of one variable from the known value of another. For example, suppose that in a certain part of the City of London rentals achieved on a certain type of office suite are recorded, together with the other costs of occupancy. These two variables, ie rental value and other costs of occupancy are then plotted on a graph to ascertain the relationship between the two, and if a reasonably straightforward relationship is found to exist in the form of a straight line (a 'line of best fit') being drawn to define this relationship, then the relationship can be used to predict rental levels on other suites, provided that the other occupancy costs are known. In practice, of course, valuation depends upon many other factors. Such an analysis taking into account a multitude of factors is known as multiple regression analysis, and can be carried out on a computer.

Where a large number of homogeneous dwellings are to be valued, as in the case of a rating revaluation, then this method may be feasible in practice. The procedure would be for features of properties, the recent sale prices of which are known, to be analysed and the results then fed into the computer with details of the sale prices. The computer would then calculate the relationship between the sale price of the property and each of the features with which the price is thought to be associated. With the results, a valuer would be able to write pattern assessment instructions, which the computer could then use for a mass valuation of all properties of a similar pattern. The Inland Revenue has already conducted a pilot study in this country, and the method is in use in the USA for Land Tax valuation and in other countries.

For more individual valuations, including valuation for investment purposes, there is likely to be healthy scepticism surrounding the use of these methods. Such methods may be used as a check on the more intuitive methods. Any such statistical backup to valuations is surely useful, either where a valuation has to be justified in negotiation, or to a board of directors, or before a Court, for example.

More sophisticated is the *Expert System*. This does not rely on the purely mathematical relationships between physical characteristics of properties and their values. It is more able to simulate the normal valuation process by being able to cope with generalities and rules of thumb. It can explain its reasoning and defend its solution in the manner of a human expert.[2]

Forecasting

Although valuers are primarily concerned with the prices at which properties change hands as evidence on which to base their valuations, there may be circumstances in which they, like their investing clients, have to make more explicit predictions about the future. It is, therefore, considered relevant to consider, albeit briefly, some of the aids to forecasting and some of the problems associated therewith.

The simplest form of forecasting is *trend forecasting* which merely extrapolates past trends into the future. This may be acceptable where a simple problem is under consideration and where relevant conditions are relatively stable. It is insufficiently sophisticated in the field of investment analysis and valuation, but it does highlight an important element in any form of forecasting. This is an understanding of the relevant system and the chains of cause and effect which have occurred in the past.

In an overview of forecasting, Brian Pearce[3] suggested that there are a number of key decisions which will indicate the forecasting method to use. The methods may be subjective versus objective. Subjective methods use processes not explicitly specified by the researcher. There are also naïve versus causal methods. Naïve methods, for instance, use historic patterns to project into the future while causal methods go beyond the variable of interest to ask why? Finally, there are linear versus classification methods.

Without wishing to go into great detail in the approaches, the resultant analysis can be grouped as follows:

Method	*Forecasting Techniques*
Subjective	Judgemental
Objective – naïve	Extrapolation
Objective – causal – linear	Econometric
Objective – causal – classification	Segmentation

Risk and Uncertainty

In statistics, *risk* relates to a situation where a probability or weight can be assigned to a possible outcome arising from a decision, while *uncertainty* is the situation when the likelihoods of the outcome are unknown, and hence no measure of probability can be made. Any predictions involve risk or uncertainty because the future is uncertain. Therefore, apart from making a prediction about what is most likely to occur in the future, it may be desirable to predict how likely it is that an event will occur in relation to the likelihood of other events occurring.

These types of prediction, implicit in management and investment decisions, are frequently made by management in the light of long experience. Where a small company is concerned, a simple approach may be fully justifiable, but where large companies or institutions are proposing to tie up large amounts of capital for long periods of time, a more rigorous approach may be desirable. This may be particularly so where committees have to make decisions and they require a well thought-out range of alternatives and possible future results of their decisions. Such a refining process may to some extent overcome the problems associated with a manager's personal attitude towards risk.

In the case of a DCF appraisal, estimates have to be made of the future cash flows. Effort is needed to avoid an unduly optimistic or pessimistic prediction of these flows. If there is a strong possibility that the cash flows will not be achieved for a particular project, it is sometimes argued that this should be allowed for by raising the criterion rate of interest to cover the risk. Such a raising of the rate of interest will to some extent be arbitrary, and in these circumstances it may be more desirable for management to consider the range of possible outcomes and the likelihood of each being achieved.

Risk is related to return but it is important to distinguish between risk and uncertainty. Whereas risk can be assessed in terms of its probability and therefore insured against or allowed for, this is not possible with uncertainty. Risk also needs to be distinguished in its application to an individual asset or to a portfolio of assets. Risk relating to a portfolio is more concerned with investment strategy and portfolio analysis and this is discussed later.

Allowance for risk can be applied in a number of ways. Firstly, it can be applied to the discount rate used in the calculation, or, secondly, it can be applied to the cashflow which arises from the investment. In the first case, for instance, if a risk-free rate is 5% and the risk premium is 2% then this premium could be added to the risk-free rate to give a discount rate of 7% which is therefore appropriate for the risk taken. If the risk is applied to the cashflow, then this flow has to be varied within a range of acceptable values and thus the output of the calculation can be assessed accordingly. The result can be found by using a statistical analysis assigning probability to the incidence of the cash flows and thus the result can even be more accurately defined.

In the simplest form, probability estimates may be made to identify the best outcome, the worst outcome, and the most likely outcome of a decision. Probability estimates may be useful to an organisation wishing to balance high-risk projects with low-risk projects. One particular project may have a high chance of making a large profit, but an equally high chance of making a loss. Such projects may need to be balanced with those having a high chance of making a small profit, with little chance of a loss. The final decision will depend upon the investor/manager's attitude towards risk or the risk which his organisation can afford to take. For example, a major loss possibility in a high-risk project might place the whole company at risk, and be one which, despite the probabilities, it could not afford to take.

There are three basic attitudes towards risk:

(i)   ignore it;
(ii)   express it verbally; or
(iii) express it numerically.

Valuers and investors have often in the past been guilty of ignoring it, or 'allowing for it' in an inevitably fairly arbitrary way through the choice of capitalisation rate. A verbal expression is imprecise: a 'risky investment' may mean anything from 5% to 95% probability of success. Following this brief introduction to the subject, the reader is advised to refer to one of the standard statistical texts for a full understanding of probability estimates, which are considered to be beyond the scope of this book.

A *decision tree* is a diagram showing the likely future course of events emanating from a given situation. As there is likely to be more than one possible course of events, the tree develops branches relating to these. These branches might develop at different points of time in the future and the particular course of events designated by each branch may be assigned a probability. A good example of the practical use of such a statistical aid in valuation might be with regard to a valuation of a leasehold or freehold interest, taking account of tenants' rights under the Landlord and Tenant Acts. For example, if a tenant's lease expires two years hence, then the likelihood of him obtaining a new lease and the likely length of that lease, or of the possibility of the landlord obtaining possession for his own use or for demolition etc could all be illustrated diagrammatically on a decision tree, with probabilities being assigned to the various possible outcomes. A suitably weighted valuation could accordingly be used if required.

Sensitivity Analysis

A forecast is sensitive to changes in the assumptions of which that forecast is based. Thus an investment decision which necessarily takes into account all relevant future events as forecast would be sensitive to a change, for example, in the assumptions relating to the likelihood of the asset being sold and capital gains tax being incurred, or to the likelihood of existing laws and taxation structure remaining substantially the same in the foreseeable future, or to the possibility of a change of government.

Such changes in assumptions may affect the whole investment decision generally, or they may affect one element in the decision such as the correct discount rate or the most likely cash flows or rate of growth. The degree to which the outcome of the decision will be affected by such changes may be analysed by a process known as a sensitivity analysis.

As with other techniques considered in this chapter, sensitivity analysis involves looking into the future. Fortunately, though the process of discounting – and the higher the rate of interest, the more this is true – more weight is attached to the near future than to the distant future. Thus, the further one has to look into the future, and thus the more difficult forecasting becomes, the smaller the effect of altering the assumptions on the outcome of the decision.

As there are a large number of factors affecting the outcome of a decision, and a large number of changes which could occur in these factors, it is first of all necessary to narrow these down to the most important factors and the most likely range of possible changes.

The factors that are considered to be sensitive over a determined range are known as *state variables* and are built into the estimate on the basis of their estimated probabilities. The remaining factors, which are not considered to be so sensitive over a determined range and are therefore constants, are known as *control variables*.

In valuations, sensitivity analysis is particularly useful in those types of valuations where there are many inputs and the effect of altering inputs on the final result can be tested through this statistical aid. An obvious example is the residual valuation, but the method could also be applied to, for example, leasehold valuations, where the effects of changing the remunerative rate, accumulative rate etc, could be tested.

Examples of approaches to sensitivity analysis include:

Simple Sensitivity Testing

Here the individual variables are changed one at a time and the effect of these changes on the result is seen. Percentage changes in the result or output can be seen relative to the changes in the input variables.

Scenario Testing

This involves changing a combination of a number of inputs and the output is then calculated with this combination of changes. This can be done in a number of ways, for instance a combination of factors which are the expected variables can be used, for instance the expected rental and yield of a future deal. In addition to this expected or realistic outcome, an optimistic scenario and a pessimistic scenario taking more optimistic or less optimistic outcomes can also be assessed.

Probability

In a more sophisticated form of sensitivity analysis, probability can be taken into account. This assesses the probability of the inputs being at a certain level and therefore can provide an even more sophisticated result. The probabilities are assigned to the input variables according to how likely these variables will be at certain levels. For instance, if there is a 50% chance of the rent being say £12 per square foot, then the probability is assigned at 0.5 and included in the calculation accordingly. By running a computer program with the assigned probabilities which picks up the inputs on the basis of the probability, for instance, of a 50% chance or picking a rent of £12, then by running the program a number of times, an average output can be assessed. This approach is called a Monte Carlo simulation. (For more information on Sensitivity Analysis, see Darlow[4] and Byrne and Cadman.[5])

Model Building and Simulation

It should be appreciated that most investment decisions involve a great range of possible values for each variable, and a large number of variables. It is in these situations that simulation techniques such as the *Monte Carlo* method may be brought into operation. This method of simulation involves a computer making a number of runs over the data and results being printed in the form of a frequency distribution table, thereby building up a model of the investment. The decision maker then has a range of most likely results to use in his final analysis.

Simulation techniques in the investment decision-making process are normally applied to DCF appraisals, where the value and timing of future individual cash-flows are likely to be difficult to determine. In the field of property investment, simulation methods are most likely to be of use in connection with residual valuations of development projects. This is because there are a large number of possible outcomes for each variable. These variables might include projected rental levels and yields, construction costs and professional fees, bridging finance, and the time taken to construct, let and/or sell the completed project.

Expert Systems

Expert systems are models and simulations which are at the leading edge of sophistication. These models and simulations attempt to copy decision-making processes in certain contexts by asking questions of the data provided, in the same way that an enquiring professional might. This process simulates the thought and decision-making processes of the brain so that appropriate responses are made in the same way. Expert systems, if appropriately modelled, can avoid subjectivity of some decision-making and appraisal. On the other hand, there is no allowance for subjectivity and wider consideration which may improve the quality of the decision made.

References and Notes

1 Kirkwood, J. 'What do Surveyors Need to Know', 269EG918.
2 Gronow, S. and Scott, I. 'Expert Systems and Multiple Regression Analysis', 278EG694.
3 Pearce, B. 'Forecasting: An Overview', in *The Application of Forecasting Techniques to the Property Market*, RICS/SPR Seminars, Spring, 1989.
4 Darlow, C. (ed.), *Valuation and Development Appraisal*, Estates Gazette, London, 1988.

5 Byrne, P. and Cadman, D. *Risk, Uncertainty and Decision-making in Property Development*, E & FN Spon, London, 1984.

Further Reading

Dixon, T. 'Getting Logged In', *Chartered Surveyor Weekly*, 6.10.88.
Kirkwood, J.S. *Information Technology and Land Administration*, Estates Gazette, 1984.
Moroney, M.J. 'Micro-computers in valuations', 277EG79.

Chapter Thirteen

Investment Strategy

Institutional Investment

The most influential investing funds in the UK, and those about whom most is known, are the *institutions* and in particular the pension funds and insurance companies.

Investment by pension funds may be broadly divided between segregated funds and pooled funds. The former relates to a separate portfolio of investments held by a particular fund, usually the larger type of fund, and the pooled fund which generally suits the smaller fund involves the acquisition of units in an investment fund, the value of the units fluctuating in line with the market value of the underlying investments.

The importance of the institutions in the investment world was underlined by the setting up of the committee to review the functioning of financial institutions (the Wilson Committee). There had been some concern that the institutions were not necessarily acting in the national interests in their mode of investment. However, pension funds are governed primarily by trust law. There is a tradition of involvement by professional investment advisors. Generally, however, there is an in-built conservatism in institutional investment. It must be recognised that there may well be a conflict between political considerations and sound investment judgment.

The Effects of Taxation

Pension funds are free from all income tax, corporation tax and capital gains tax liability. The position of the insurance companies is that as regards their life assurance business, the excess of investment income and capital gains over management expenses are subject to a special corporation tax rate and their pension business is totally exempt. With regard to their general annuity business, if income and gains are all paid over to the annuitants, no tax is payable by the company. The influence of the institutions in the prime property investment market has been stressed throughout this book, and the steadily increasing flow of pension fund contributions as a result of higher incomes has continued the trend of institutional investment in property and made for the pressure of funds in this and other avenues of investment. Over the last decade the proportion of institutional funds directed into property has rarely been outside the range of 10–20% of the total.

Pension funds have a tax advantage in acquiring leasehold investments, and particularly short leaseholds, in that they have no need to set aside an amount of income for sinking fund instalment which is gross of tax nor to allow for the tax normally payable on the interest on sinking fund accumulations. Despite this advantage, institutions are nevertheless very interested in freehold investment because of the need to plan long term and achieve long-term growth and partly to avoid the risk associated with some leasehold investments.

The disadvantage of property shares as an investment to the non-tax paying institution is that the earnings of the company are subject to corporation tax whereas direct investment will relieve the investor of this burden. It also follows that trading activity such as partnerships, joint venture companies and leasing must be designed so as to minimise the effect of tax on the fund.

Portfolio management has equally important tax implications for the *high rate taxpayer*. As capital gains tax is only paid when an asset is sold (and a chargeable gain is made thereon) and as there is an element of a realised capital gain which is tax free, then, a capital gain may be better than an income for high rate taxpayers. This is reflected in the preference of such investors for reversionary investments providing a low initial income but with a proportionately high capital appreciation. Such investors are likely to be averse to short leaseholds for the reason of the effect of taxation on sinking funds. Investments which provide various tax attractions such as owner-occupied houses, industrial investment, some capital transfer relief for working farmers, will all be sought out and used to full advantage by well-advised taxpayers.

Gilt-edged stocks are completely free of Capital Gains Tax if held for more than one year. Generally, stocks with low coupon rates are purchased by higher-rate taxpayers who are buying for capital gain, while those with high coupon rates are attractive to standard-rate taxpayers, insurance company life funds, pension funds and charities, all of whom enjoy favourable or zero rating for tax purposes.

The real rate of return enjoyed by the investor can be calculated in two ways. First, by expressing the coupon rate as a rate of return on purchase price; second, by taking account of any capital gain or loss if held to redemption and calculating the redemption yield. Because of differences in tax liability between investors, these yields are frequently assessed before allowance for tax and expressed as gross redemption yields. Specific investors should also assess their individual net redemption yields in order to select the most suitable stock for them to acquire.

Portfolio Policy

An investment portfolio is the complete list of investments held by a particular investing fund. Portfolio management has been defined by H.R. Jenkins, director of the Coal Board Pension Fund, as being:

> 'A continuous process of reviewing the portfolio to determine the areas where action can be taken with a view to improving the return from an investment.
>
> A restless activity involving:
> (a) Analysing each investment property and comparing its actual performance against the expectations on acquisition and its comparison with other forms of investment in the portfolio;
> (b) Seeking ways and means of improving the performance of a particular investment;
> (c) Disposing of investments where long term prospects are likely to be less than expected.'

A fund's investment policy will depend upon a number of factors. The following list is by no means exhaustive and some of the factors listed are interrelated:

(i)   The fund's liquidity position.
(ii) The size of the fund.
(iii) The level of risk which the fund's managers consider acceptable.
(iv) Any special considerations, eg:
    (a) A preference for income or growth. Many charities may prefer immediate income at the possible expense of growth.
    (b) A preference for UK investment or overseas investment.
    (c) Life insurance companies are to an extent influenced by the bonus rate on 'with profits' policies.
(v)   The fund's tax position.

Such a policy should be flexible enough to respond to changing market conditions, and having established a policy, management can concentrate on investing judiciously within that framework. For the institutions, and the insurance companies in particular, management is likely to be largely a matter of decision-making with regard to new investments. However, if a policy is to be carried through and advantage taken of market situations, managing the existing portfolio – switching from one investment medium to another – is equally important.

A fund may be set up to mirror as closely as possible an index such as the Financial Times Index. Such funds are highly diversified. Some funds split their portfolios between *active* and *passive management* sections. Active management should produce better results but is more expensive and troublesome. In passing, it may be noted that in a very efficient market such as the stock market some commentators observe that any amount of investment analysis cannot produce substantially improved performance as all advantages and disadvantages of particular investments are already discounted in their market prices.

Other aspects of active property portfolio management include the judicious buying and selling of properties, and the balancing of the portfolio. For example, a combination of leasehold interests and freehold reversionary investments might help to provide a continuation of income flow. Restructuring of leases, for example, to put a lease on full repairing and insuring terms or to update the period of rent reviews may be undertaken by negotiation with the tenant. Refurbishment, for example when a lease falls in, may provide enhanced return on capital. Acquisition or disposal of an interest may release *marriage value*. An instance of a disposal in such a situation would be to the tenant, as where long-term prospects have become less good than before. Marriage value, ie the release of potential value arising through the merger of interests, is illustrated in the following example.

Example 12.1

The fund owns the ground lease of a prime office investment underlet to a substantial tenant on a 25-year lease with five-year reviews at the net rack rent of £25,000 per annum. The ground rent is geared to the rack rent as a constant proportion of 20%, and the lease has 85 years to run. The fund is considering buying the freehold interest.

Value of leasehold interest	
Profit rent	£20,000
YP 85 years @ 7% and 4%	13.99
Capital value, say	£279,800

Value of freehold interest

Rent reserved		£5,000
YP perp. @ 5.5% (reversion ignored as being too remote)		18.1818
Capital value, say		£90,900

Gain on marriage

Rack rent	net pa	£25,000
YP perp. @ 6%		16.6667
Value of married interests		£416,700
Less leasehold value	£279,800	
freehold value	90,900	£370,700
Gain on marriage		£46,000

Notes

(i)   Although actuarially there is little difference between a freehold interest and an 85-year lease, the latter is normally regarded as a considerably less attractive investment and this is reflected in the YP adopted in the leasehold valuation.

(ii) The gain on marriage is likely to have to be split between the parties to the transaction either on a 50:50 basis, in proportion to the value of their respective interests, or according to their relative bargaining strengths.

(iii) Cost of merger (legal and surveyors' fees) might have to be allowed against the gain on marriage, and these would depend to some extent upon the apportionment of gain between the parties.

Various *sectors of the investment market* are now considered.

Apart from shareholding, the other major means of investing in industry is through fixed interest *debentures*. This type of investment became unpopular due to the lack of willingness of borrowers to commit themselves to long-term obligations at high interest rates and lenders' reluctance to be exposed to the threat of negative real returns. The choice now among investing funds is between gilts and equities (apart from property and other forms of investment). There have been experiments with growth debentures, such as a short-term debenture carrying a lower than market interest rate with an extra payment to be made related to growth and turnover.

Pension funds should obviously aim to keep pace with inflation because the pensions that they are eventually required to pay out will be based upon the then earnings of the individual which will of course have been affected by inflation over the years up to that date. However, there are various reasons why it may be desirable for funds to invest in fixed interest securities and in particular *gilt-edged stock*. Funds do not normally have liquidity problems, but any particular liquidity requirement which can be anticipated may be covered by investing in gilts.

Different funds invest in government stock with different lives according to the estimated life of their liabilities. Insurance companies for example are likely to accept a 15-year life while pension funds may go for longer, say 25 years, unless they are undertaking a more precise matching of liabilities. Undated stocks are unlikely to be used. These are now regarded as a fairly specialist type of investment and the amount of stocks available is now relatively small.

Gilt-edged stock is less *volatile* than equities and hence incorporation of such stocks into a portfolio will tend to mitigate the volatile effects of equities. In times of fluctuating interest rates it is possible to make substantial profits by active dealing in the gilt-edged market. They are extremely marketable and the expenses of dealing are low. Active management of gilts is therefore essential. These comments relate mainly to the larger issues of gilt-edged stocks. The gilt-edged market includes many stocks, not only those issued by the British government, but also issued by local authorities, Commonwealth governments, electricity, gas and transport stocks, and some of the smaller ones may be less marketable. Within the larger issues, however, there is still a vast range of maturity dates and undated stock.

If the government wishes to raise more money or if a previous issue of stock has just expired, then a new stock (*tap stock*) will be issued. Large tap issues will have to provide some inducement for new investors to participate or for existing investors to switch, and it is for this reason that some stocks are often cheaper than others.

An example is the gilt-edged *index-linked stock*. The issue was made of a 2% stock. This means that the return will consist of the annual coupon of 2% plus the rate of inflation using the retail price index eight months in arrears. The reason for this is so that throughout the stock's life the amount of the next dividend payment and final redemption value will be known six months in advance. This form of investment is generally welcome and will provide a basis for comparison in the implied acceptable real rates of return on investment. In some quarters it is considered that the index-linked gilt will become a yardstick for measurement of property performance.

Investment Analysis

Institutions' equity holdings tend to concentrate on companies with large market capitalisation. These are likely to provide more secure investments, but unlikely to provide the spectacular growth which may be associated with higher risk new companies. Pension funds tend to diversify their shares and increasingly include an element of overseas holdings. This diversification will tend to reduce the effect of the volatility associated with the equity market. Diversification reduces risk. It is necessary for an investor to choose the risk class in which he proposes to invest and then maximise the returns within that class. There are two ends of the spectrum with regard to investment policy. There is a confident forecasting policy, whereby the investor believes he can beat the market, or at the other extreme, no confidence in forecasting policy and a following of a market index. The larger the portfolio, the more it will be influenced by the market. A portfolio is well diversified if 95% of its variation is explained by the market. Generally, retail properties are more volatile than offices or industrial, due to factors such as their variation in location and type. Retail properties tend to produce higher growth.

As opposed to properties, stocks follow the market closely. No passive investment strategy is possible with property. Property portfolios are not highly diversified. However, most of the risk in such a portfolio can be diversified away by increasing the size of the portfolio. *Risk* equates to the variability (or volatility) of annual or total returns.

As regards risk in equity investment, there are basically three types of risk which are to some extent independent of one another. These are the volatility of the whole equity market; that of the particular industry; and that of the individual company. Portfolio managers have to steer the middle course of minimising risk through a sufficient spread of shares and yet avoiding an indifferent performance by spreading out too far and too thinly. Diversification can reduce *specific risk* relating to company or industry, but not general *market risk* sometimes known as *systematic risk*.

It is a basic rule in the equity market to buy when the bottom of a trough is reached and a bull market is to follow – assuming this can be correctly anticipated! A more subtle rule relates to the volatility of a particular stock. The historic volatility of a stock in fluctuating markets has been measured by what is known as the *Beta factor*, the average volatility of all stocks analysed being given a value of unity; or alternatively, as a standard deviation of returns. Thus, if a manager is sufficiently in touch with the market and it is moving up, he should switch into highly volatile stocks (ie those with a high Beta factor) as these are likely to respond more than average. Conversely, if the market is moving down, he should switch into those with a low Beta factor as they will be least affected by such a fall.

As regards *gilt-edged stock*, if a stock is dated, the government promise to redeem at the original or nominal value at a given date or within a given range of dates. In the latter cases, they will choose the moment they consider to be most advantageous to them in terms of market interest rates prevailing at the time. The overall yield taking into account income and capital gain or loss on a dated stock is the *redemption yield*.

Example 12.2

Calculate by DCF the gross redemption yield on government stock issued at 16% with redemption in three years and selling at £15 above par (ie face or nominal value).

The calculation is given below. In this case the income flow is on a half-yearly in arrears basis. In year 3 there will be a half-year's income together with the redemption value at par. It is also possible and useful to calculate the net-of-tax return to a taxpaying investor.

Year	Cash Flow	PV £1 @ 10%	Present Value	PV £1 @ 11%	Present Value
½	8	0.953	7.62	0.949	7.59
1	8	0.909	7.27	0.901	7.21
1½	8	0.867	6.94	0.855	6.84
2	8	0.826	6.61	0.812	6.50
2½	8	0.788	6.30	0.770	6.16
3	8 } = 108 100 }	0.751	81.11	0.731	78.95
			115.84		113.25
	Less price		115		115
	NPV		+ 0.84		−1.75
	IRR 10 +		0.84		
			0.84	+1.75	
		= 10.32%			

In carrying out these calculations particular care must be exercised when stocks have a spread of redemption dates. If the price is below par it is customary to calculate the yield assuming maturity at the end of the range of dates, if above par the beginning date is taken.

One method of analysis of a gilt-edged market involves the use of the *yield curve*. This relates the pattern of redemption yields to the maturities of the respective stocks. In stable conditions, most investors prefer stocks with a shorter life given the same redemption yield and this will show up on the yield curve. The reason for this preference is fairly obvious. Suppose interest rates have risen from 10% to 20% since the issue of an un-dated stock. That stock would have fallen in value from £100 to £50. If, on the other hand, that stock was dated one year hence, the price would only need to fall to around £90 to leave the investor with a 20% return comprising £10 income for the year and £10 capital gain on redemption.

The demand for low *coupon* stocks by taxpayers results in these stocks producing a lower gross redemption yield than high coupon stocks of similar term and account is taken of this in analysis by yield curve. Generally, the longer the outstanding term of the stock, the greater its volatility, but for a given term to redemption, low coupon stocks are normally more volatile than high coupon. A stock with a coupon of 10% for example, and five years to run, currently selling for its nominal value of £100, will show a yearly return of 10%. For the return (taking account of both income and capital growth over the next five years) to rise to 20%, the price of the stock would have to fall by about 28% to £72. But if the coupon was only 2%, the stock would have to be selling for around £71 now to give a yearly return of 10%. For this return to rise to 20%, the price of the stock would have to fall by around 32% to £48 or so.

Portfolio Performance Measurement

The *historic redemption yield* is the rate at which the historic net cash flow and latest capital value of the property must be discounted in order to equate to the original purchase cost of the investment. To analyse a portfolio in this way it is necessary to aggregate the costs and rental flows and valuations from the various properties within the portfolio. The *historic revenue yield* should be differentiated from the historic redemption yield. The historic revenue yield is computed in a similar way to the historic redemption yield, but excludes any capital gains or losses. Hence it solely measures the historic net income flow.

The Richard Ellis Analytical Consultancy Unit provided a glossary of terms relating to property analysis and this helped the analysis of properties and portfolios of properties in various ways. This firm has also undertaken research into property capital performance.[1] This work investigates the intrinsic growth of reversionary investments and distinguishes three elements in capital growth and enables a consideration of the quality of capital growth to be determined. Questions of capital sensitivity and gearing are investigated. Thus changes in capital value may arise due to (i) a change in the estimated rental value; (ii) a change in the investment yield; and (iii) the approach of the next rent review. Thus, higher quality capital growth resulting from underlying increases in the rental value of the investment may be distinguished from other factors such as the mere factor of the next rent review drawing nearer.

Many of the major firms of chartered surveyors now produce rental or capital value property indices, in some cases based upon a sample of actual institutional investment performance. In many instances, comparisons are also drawn between performance of property investment as against other forms of investment on the basis of these indices. While providing broad general historic trends, these indices, notwithstanding their statistical validity or otherwise, may or may not provide a good basis for forecasting future performance. The compilation and publication of rental and capital value indices for property is a recent phenomenon, and those organisations which have attempted it are to be congratulated for their pioneering spirit alone. However, the compilation of such an index is beset with many difficulties, many of which are now being realised.

The stock market is an efficient market, producing reliable and regular data upon which to base an index of investment performance such as the FTA all-share index. This is in stark contrast to the property market, the inefficiencies and heterogeneity of which are outlined in the opening chapters of this book. If a hypothetical portfolio is to be formed, for example, the problem arises as to which types of property are to be included and the weighting between them. The FTA index, on the other hand, includes all shares, not merely prime investments. Further, the variety of terms which can attach to a deal other than the bare rental or price produce difficulties for those seeking to obtain relevant data. When evidence is as sparse as it was in the property market collapse of 1974 for example, it may even be argued that there is virtually no market at all, and in these circumstances an index, whether based on actual transactions or on valuations, may be particularly suspect.

Insignia Richard Ellis have produced a monthly bulletin similar in many respects to a Broker's circular. The index sets out to provide a fast and frequent market barometer registering investor and occupier sentiment towards property. It is not intended for long-term performance comparison, nor is it intended as a yardstick against which fund performance should be measured. Until now, there has been nothing comparable with the FT/Actuary's indices and up-to-date indications of market trends are needed to make property decisions. The index charts the movement of portfolios on a month-to-month basis in total capital and rent returns.

The National Association of Pension Funds (NAPF) has doubts about valuation-based measures as against transaction-based measures such as the Stock Market indices. In view of the potential conflicts of interests amongst those supplying the information who are also prominent in the sale and letting of commercial properties, the RICS has investigated the problem.

Investors require to know three main factors, which are as follows:

(a) A breakdown of past performance and in particular, how each property has performed, how the portfolio has compared with competitors' portfolios, and how property has performed compared with other forms of investment within the portfolio.

Measurement of past performance will include calculations of past returns from the portfolio and identification of the components of the portfolio performance.

(b) Information to help in the day-to-day running of the portfolio, including an identification of the economic indicators which should be monitored, factors affecting performance, and assessment of future movements in these factors.

(c) Knowledge as to how to improve future performance with regard to the best time to invest in property, the proportion of new money to be invested in that sector, the type and location of property to be acquired, together with iden-tification of properties to be sold, refurbished or be developed.

Improvement of future performance is obviously the key to successful portfolio management.

In comparing property and gilt-edged returns, it is necessary to examine the variables underlying investors target rates of return. The first group of these factors determine the gross rate of return – transaction costs, management costs and taxation.

With regard to *transaction costs*, property is substantially more expensive to transact than the same value gilt-edged stock, but a factor which must be borne in mind is the long term nature of property as an investment. It will be bought and sold far less frequently than stocks and shares. The second factor relates to *management costs*. Costs of management of property are undoubtedly greater than those relating to gilts. As concerns *taxation*, gilts are exempt from Capital Gains Tax if held for over 12 months. This is generally irrelevant in making a comparison, however, as gilts are essentially non-growth investments. It can be argued that property, in fact, has a tax advantage over gilts in that the return from gilts is entirely in the form of income, which is all taxable, whereas the total returns from property are part income (taxable) and part growth (non-taxable), unless sold and with the gain indexed.

The second group of variables determine the net return – risk, liquidity and marketability. As concerns liquidity and marketability, property is clearly at a disadvantage. It has been argued that this latter disadvantage is offset by the net advantages of property with regard to the first group of variables. Partly by portfolio diversification, the risks between the various sectors of the investment market can be evened out. It has been argued that as the capital values of gilts vary considerably over time, they are in fact more volatile than property as an investment, and in this sense should not be considered as being more secure.[2]

In carrying out portfolio analysis, it is necessary to analyse the whole portfolio, sectors within the portfolio and, finally, individual properties. Properties can be compared with the market by regression analysis. Sensitivity analysis can also be used to identify the effect of changes in various factors affecting the portfolio.[3]

Portfolio Analysis

There are two areas of financial theory which have had some impact in the areas of property investment valuation and appraisal and these areas relate to market efficiency and the capital asset pricing model.

Market Efficiency

Market efficiency theories as applied to property markets say that the price of property investments should reflect all available information in the market. Dealers in the market should recognise when prices are out of line and accordingly will make a profit by buying or selling and thus driving the price back to equilibrium values consistent with all available information. Thus, in an efficient market, property will be traded at the correct prices. This situation will provide confidence to the investors involved and ensure the best economic allocation of funds.

It is likely that the property market is efficient in what is described as a weak form level which means that the market reflects the past history of prices and is efficient in respect of these. It may not, however, use all the information available as signified by higher levels of efficiency called strong forms. As access to market information becomes more restricted, it is likely that the market will become progressively more inefficient so there is more likelihood of dealers earning abnormal returns.

Gerald Brown[4] suggests that the efficiency of the market is difficult to test with valuation models which are based on the comparison method. Although this method does give a guide to the potential price in the market-place, it does not indicate as to whether the property is under- or over-priced in its economic sense (that is relative to future income and risk). Conventional evaluation models are thus unable to answer this question as they have no economic reference to market equilibrium.

Capital Asset Pricing Model (CAPM)

The CAPM as developed in capital market theory helps us to understand the relationships of risk and return in an investment. The CAPM can give us an indication of how to measure risk. If the risk is related to a single property asset, it relates to the variability of returns and this is measured statistically by their variants or standard deviation. As applied to risk in a portfolio of properties, we are interested here in the contribution of a property to the overall risk of the entire portfolio. Because a property's variance in return is dispersed in a large diversified portfolio, the single property's variance no longer represents its contribution to the risk of a large portfolio. In this case, contribution is measured by the property's covariance with the other properties in the portfolio. For instance, if a property has high returns when the overall return of the portfolio is low and vice versa, the property has a negative covariance with the portfolio. It acts as a hedge against risk by reducing the risk of the portfolio. If the property has a higher positive covariance, there is a high risk for the investor.

In the CAPM the measure of risk is called Beta. The criteria for holding an investment in a portfolio can be defined in terms of the property's Beta. Investors will only hold a risky property if its expected return is high enough to compensate for its risk. There is thus a trade-off between the risk and the reward of future income. The expected return on a property is positively related to the property's Beta or risk. The model gives the formula that the expected return on an asset for a period is equal to the riskless rate of return plus a variable which reflects risk. This variable is Beta multiplied by the difference between the expected return on the market portfolio minus the risk-free rate. Beta here is the systematic risk. This systematic risk is still borne after achieving full diversification.

Cost of Capital

The analysis of the CAPM can be combined with the notion of the contribution of debt and equity finance in the purchase costs for the asset. This then provides some background to gearing which is the relationship of debt capital to total capital in the purchase of the property asset. As debt returns are usually defined by the provider of debt whereas equity return is a surplus, this form of analysis can more clearly define the actual returns on property by differentiating between the debt and equity returns.

References

1 Sykes, S. *Property Capital Performance – A New Approach*, Richard Ellis Analytical Consultancy Unit, December 1980.
2 Fraser, W. 'Gilt yields and property's target return', 273EG1291.
3 Hetherington, J. 'Property Performance Measurement Systems', 271EG260.
4 Brown, G. *Property Investment and the Market*, E & FN Spon, 1991, p. 80.

Further Reading

Barber, C. 'Performance Evaluation', EG Issue 8834.
Bowie, N. 'Depreciation: Who Hoodwinked Whom?' 262EG405.
Brown, G. 'Explaining portfolio performance', 276EG1335.
Brown, G. 'Making Property Investment Decisions via Capital Market Theory', *Journal of Valuation*, Vol. 2, No. 2.
Chapman, H., Wyatt, A. and Thompson, J. 'Measuring Property Performance', *Chartered Surveyor*, May 1980.
Fraser, W. 'Property's risk and the enigma of yield trends in the 1980s', 277EG706.
Greenwell, W. & Co. *Property Indices*, 1978.
Hall, P.O. 'Alternative Approaches to Performance Measurement', 255EG935.
Mason, L.R. 'Performance Measurement', 256EG109.
Merrett, A.J. *Valuation of Ordinary Shares*, Gower Press, 1970.
Patrick, M.J. 'What Use is Property Performance Analysis?' *Journal of Valuation*, Vol. 2, No. 2.
Patrick, M.J. 'An Argument for Performance Measurement and Analysis', 263EG641.
Ward, C. 'The Evaluation of Risk', 260EG253.

Chapter Fourteen

An Overview

Introduction

By the mid-1980s property had fallen into disfavour as a channel for investment for institutions. The institutions in this context are broadly represented by the Pension Funds and Insurance Companies which have generally accounted for over 80% of property investment in recent years.

In the late 1970s property became less popular as an investment channel, particularly with the advent of the Index-Linked Gilt which provided an alternative secure and inflation-proof form of investment.

From an average figure of 19% of institutional investment held in property in the late 1970s, the proportion fell to approximately 8% in 1986 and in fact was at this relatively low level for much of the 1980s.

The performance of property relative to equities began to improve in 1987 and this trend was accelerated by the crash on the stock market in October of that year now generally referred to as 'Black Monday'.

Typically, half or more of investment properties held by institutions are offices, one quarter shops, and the remainder mainly industrial with a very small proportion of agricultural and other properties. While property as a whole has typically remained at 10% or less of the total investment portfolio, equities have represented perhaps 40% and fixed interest securities around 30%. The percentage held in property by the end of 1992 was estimated at 7%.[1]

The period 1990–1999 was a period of recession, low inflation, globalisation and subsequent stability. By the end of the decade, the property market appeared stable.

Offices

The effects of 'Black Monday' in the city office market in 1987 were to see some dampening of demand due to the low volume of trading in the city. 1987 also saw the 'big bang' or revolution in working practices in the city. A number of foreign companies sought to establish themselves in the city, particularly the Japanese for whom occupancy costs here were lower than in Tokyo. The same cannot be said for European companies for whom the city of London represented the highest occupancy costs in Europe. Nonetheless, further demand from these sources occurred following European economic unification in 1992. Between 1986 and 1988 there had been substantial increases in office values, ranging from approximately 80% in the city to 120% in Holborn, in addition to a slight drop in yields in 1988 for the first time since 1980. Some of the original 1850 offices are still in use and approximately 80% of the stock is pre-1970, putting pressure on new development.

The increase of obsolescence in office buildings is a point investors are likely to have to take more account of in the future. The Jones Lang Wootton survey indicates that offices lose 2.7% of their appeal per annum in comparison with new buildings. The research reports will be useful to fund managers in planning refurbishments.

The stock of offices in the city built up after 1988 and the market became very difficult. By 1994 a continued take-up had reduced office space available.[2]

Traditional town centre offices have been the worst performing sector over 40 years. This is in part because tenants have required considerable improvements in the technical specification, layout and appearance of buildings. Depreciation and obsolescence have badly affected performance as occupiers' needs have changed and flexibility of layout and services has become the key issue.

Shops

As in the industrial and office sectors, there was a growth in rents in 1988 of well over 20%. Nevertheless, yields were at an 11-year high. This apparent anomaly is probably explained by the market looking back to poor previous rental growth which particularly occurred in the early to mid-1980s. Prime Oxford Street rents fell between 1980 and 1982.

While there are short-term factors which indicate poor rental growth in the immediate future, the underlying health of the retail sector appears good. While retail sales grew at less than 2% per annum through the 1970s, this increased to 4% per annum in the early 1980s and over 5% per annum in the late 1980s. This was partly a reflection of greater disposable income and partly a result of the credit card boom. Retail sales were historically high as a result of the underlying strength of the economy.

As regards out-of-town schemes, a number of these are continuing to be put forward although much loyalty remains for traditional centres. Nonetheless, the demand for retail warehouses remains high. The growth in the development of these began in the early 1980s, mainly for DIY stores at that time. Car care stores are now the predominant force in the sector. Retail development generally is at a relatively low ebb at the present time. Expansion plans have decreased over the period from 1989 with a low in 1992, but since then confidence has picked up. Retail warehousing continues to be the buoyant sector.

As concerns the geographical distribution of growth and rental levels within the UK, unlike the office and industrial sectors, there is little in the way of a north/south divide in the retail sector with individual towns and centres within all regions capable of high rents and growth. About 600 shopping centres were built between 1960 and 2000. These are typically in town centres and their values range between £20m and £100m.[3]

Industrial Property

Mainly due to the relatively rapid obsolescence of industrial buildings, yields on this form of investment have always been higher than those on shops and offices. In 1982 prime industrial yields stood at 6.25% according to the Healey & Baker Prime Yields graph. Relatively poor performance in this sector in the 1980s, however, led to an increase in yields. From 1981 to 1986 for example, total returns in the sector were under 6% per annum, easily the worst performance of the three major sectors. The main reasons were too much investment in this sector in the late 1970s to 1981, coupled with a recession. This led to a decline in capital values form 1982 to 1986. This led to very selective purchasing by the institutions with nearly 90% of acquisitions being in London and the South East.

Towards the end of the period, however, there was a complete change in fortunes in the sector and the mood is now buoyant.

Available space had fallen 50% since 1983 due to lack of investment in the sector. With average yields being nearly 10% in 1987, these have come down to about 9% with prime yields at approximately 7.5%. There were rent increases of 36% in 1988 according to the Hillier Parker Investors Chronicle Index. This meant that the industrial sector was ahead of shops and offices for the first time since 1980. Growth was somewhat less in secondary investments (buildings 15 to 20 years old) being at 27% for the year.

One particular feature of the market is the trend to owner-occupation and there is now strong demand by owner-occupiers, particularly in London and the South East. With regard to the geographical distribution of the performance of industrial property within the UK, the north/south divide widened during the 1980s but closed in the 1990s. The industrial market in 1994 had begun to pick up. For the first time since 1989, availability of space had begun to fall. Available space at April 1994 was estimated at 18 million m². Agents and researchers predict an overall decline continuing in the amount of space available.[4]

As at December 2000, King Sturge reported 13.6 million m² of industrial floorspace vacant. They suggested that the supply of good quality buildings is likely to remain modest in many locations and that average industrial yield should stay firm.[5]

Enterprise Zones

As part of the Government's initiatives to restore industry and prosperity to the depressed regions, Enterprise Zones were introduced in June 1981. Firms locating in the Enterprise Zones benefited from exemption from rates and development land tax when that was in force. They were also entitled to 100% capital allowances on corporation and income tax for commercial and industrial buildings. Planning controls were also simplified.

The exemption from rates has been for a limited period and this is liable to have an effect on rents when the period comes to an end. Various grants have been available and Urban Development Corporations have been established in some areas. Enterprise Zones are now to be generally discontinued.

Hi-Tech

The 1987 Use Classes Order introduced a separate business use (B1) allowing changes to be made between industrial and office uses. This formalised and extended a situation which had already arisen with regard to the development of business parks or hi-tech industrial parks providing superior industrial accommodation for

'Knowledge Based Industries', notably in the western corridor – the area around the M4 motorway stretching from London to Bristol – and particularly in the micro-electronics field. The development of business parks has now extended to attracting professional and other office users. Hi-tech developments are predominantly two-storey although the market has now become further sophisticated by the demand for mid-tech industrial uses with a large office element. The first breed of hi-tech accommodation is now proving difficult to let due to inadequacies of design, high site cover and other factors. There is in fact still good demand for basic sheds.

Completed developments of business parks have slowed down in a response to fears of over supply. Only 100,000 m² was completed in 1985 compared with 700,000 m² in 1980. The introduction of the 1987 Use Classes Order, however, has seen something of a reversal of the situation, with a rush to B1 construction in view of the higher rents anticipated. Planners in the Thames valley and London areas anticipate an over supply. By 1989, B1 yields were down to 6.5% to 7% with rents up to £200 per square metre. Rental growth in 1987 and 1988 had been mainly in the South although this had spread to the North and the Midlands. There were big regional differences and 50% of planned space for business parks was in the South-East. Office parks, being offices with B1 planning consent, situated outside town centres and often in 'park' schemes, showed a marked fall in rental growth in the period to 1993. By 2000 some business parks had begun to command higher rents than town centre offices.

Agricultural Properties

These have been traditionally regarded as very secure investments, although growth in the 1970s was not really sufficient to compensate for such low initial yields and the situation worsened in the 1980s where there were large falls in values in real terms. The institutions have therefore endeavoured to unload their investments in this sector. Agriculture has underperformed commercial property and speculative profit has mainly been engineered through the break-up of estates.

Market Confidence

After the 1989/1992 recession and certainly by the middle of 1993, market confidence had increased and had been shown in a number of surveys. Surveys of property lenders showed more inclination to finance non-risky property investment. In addition, by the beginning of 1994, confidence was also returning to business tenants. The Jones Lang Wootton Property Confidence Review[6] has recorded the most positive findings in business confidence since the survey began in 1969. A large majority of the companies are more confident of their short-term prospects. However, despite this renewed confidence, companies are still disposing of space, although the space shed by the companies fell from 3.6 million sq ft in the six months to July 1993 to 1.2 million sq ft in the six months to January 1994. Renewed confidence in the investment markets had lowered yields to a level at which, compared to yields for gilts, they were becoming uncompetitive. Property companies in the market had been re-rated, signifying that their market capitalisation as viewed from the share price has increased rapidly, thus enabling property investment and property trading companies to borrow more against their equity. The property market to the end of 1999 appeared financially stable. Low inflation, low interest rates and a growing economy produced total returns of 12% in 1998 and 1999.[7]

Property Research

A number of various areas of research are now being developed. Areas of research sponsored by the RICS include the relationship of business cycles to the property cycle. In addition, interest has been created by the opening of Eastern Europe and the property markets in that region. In terms of valuation principles and methods, further research has continued into portfolio valuation and the development of the existing valuation methods and these are dealt with in more detail below.

Lizieri and Richards[8] suggest that there are three categories of research into property investment that are being developed:

(i)   The development of measures of property performance at an individual property or portfolio level and in terms of a benchmark market indicator. Hence the development of commercial property indices.

(ii) The forecasting of activity at a variety of levels from macroeconomic forecasts, through national property market trends to detailed analysis at sector, region and town level.

(iii) The combination of performance measurement and the forecasting of results to establish portfolio strategies: that is the diversification of the portfolio, the management of property as a financial asset and the buy/sell decision.

Property in a Portfolio Context

The valuation of properties in a traditional way building by building is now seen as an inadequate approach as investors are exposed to localised property markets and the wide swings of local prices. Such volatility is controlled in other investment portfolios such as shares and these techniques are now being introduced to commercial property portfolios. The use of modern portfolio theory which was discussed in some detail previously has been debated at some length because of the range of possible properties and markets; the right choice for the portfolio is even more important in property than it may well be in competing investment markets like equities and gilts. The general feeling is that most property port-folios are badly diversified. Also, property portfolios demand active management unlike other investment media. If there is no active management, then the choice of properties for the portfolio might be negated anyway. The performance of a portfolio in comparison with an index is difficult to chart. Property portfolios after all need to be analysed, not only in terms of return, but also in terms of risk.[9]

Findings from the Investment Property Databank (IPD) have shown that diversification is only possible in large funds with an excess of 250 properties where patterns of performance or volatility do not deviate markedly from the market norms. However, it has been possible for small funds in the region of 30 or 40 properties to achieve higher levels of return over the last ten years or so without higher than average volatility. However, for the smaller fund such a result cannot be guaranteed. The conclusion of the IPD evidence is that the complexity of the asset class and the illiquidity of the market contribute to the difficulty of achieving low-risk, well-diversified portfolios without large and expensive asset bases.

Research into Valuation Methods

The RICS over a period commissioned a number of reports which looked into valuation methods. These included the residual valuation, the profits method, the contractor's method and reversionary valuations.

The cost approach to valuation

In a paper presented at a valuation techniques seminar on March 13 1992, Owen Connellan[10] suggested that the calculation of value on a cost basis usually concerns three categories of building. These are *precisely similar*, *simple* or *modern substitute*. He suggested that these categories be replaced by three alternative categories, being *reconstructed*, *modified reconstructed* and *radical alternative*. Depreciation is defined as the loss of the real existing use value of a capital asset. In depreciation, the age/future life method is the most commonly used method. This assumes straight line depreciation. It is generally agreed that this must be a wrong approach.

The Depreciated Replacement Cost is defined by Gross Replacement Cost (GRC) × Depreciation Factor (DF) = Net Replacement Cost (NRC).

$$DF = \frac{\text{Estimated future life of building}}{\text{Age + Estimated future life of building}} = \frac{\text{Remaining life}}{\text{Total life}}$$

The conclusion is that cost base valuations are the best available sources for *no-market* properties. However, the comment is made that the guidance notes and information papers provided by the Asset Valuation Standing Committee are not as useful as they might be, as the advice is too theoretical and does not give much practical guidance.

Profits Method

Ann Colborne presented a paper[11] at the valuation techniques seminar on the Profits Method. She suggested that there are three different approaches:

(i)   Total capitalisation
(ii) Dual capitalisation/super profit
(iii) Capitalised (discounted) earnings

The total earnings method of valuation is based on the net operating profit (profit before interest and tax) × a multiplier to give a valuation.

In the dual capitalisation method, the profit figures are taken for the last three to five years. The net profit is capitalised separately from the goodwill. The various approaches to the profit method are comparable and use the sustainable net profit for valuation. The basic differences are:

(a)   The division of the net profit as a return from the building and tenant.
(b)   A discount rate used over a limited time period as against the use of a Years' Purchase.

The valuation of reversionary freeholds

In his RICS research, Crosby[12] suggests that the major criticism of contemporary approaches is that they do not forecast growth and that they subjectively choose a discount rate. He suggests that using the implied rental growth rate analysis will reduce the subjectivity.

There is a debate between academics over which type of model makes the best use of available evidence. The growth explicit model using comparable transactions to assess an implied growth rate after subjectively choosing a discount rate or, alternatively, the growth explicit model using the objectively found equivalent yield from comparable transactions and then applying it subjectively to properties to be valued.

The view is that the subjective element in contemporary methods has less effect on the possible range of solutions than the subjective element in conventional approaches. This is still, however, a minority view. The market valuation of reversionary freehold property is generally carried out by conventional growth implicit techniques but the research showed that not all were using the same conventional approach. Crosby, in his paper, indicates that in the future he perceives a demise of the traditional term and reversion approach. These aspects have already been discussed in some detail in Chapter 9.

Depreciation and Obsolescence

The problems of depreciation and obsolescence are incorporated in the cost approach to valuation, but they are of importance generally in looking at the valuation of property in the market. Techniques can make allowance for depreciation and there have been a number of suggestions as to how this can be done. Depreciation has been defined as the measure of wearing out, consumption or other loss of value of the fixed asset whether arising from use, effluxion of time or obsolescence through technology or market changes (Bowie[13]). Depreciation can be divided into curable and incurable depreciation. Curable depreciation relates to lack of maintenance but incurable depreciation relates to obsolescence. Obsolescence can be further divided into internal obsolescence such as the wearing out of a building (the technical changes which render space useless), and external obsolescence which relate to the decay of the environment such as changes in the location of industry. It is possible to make an adjustment to the yield on a property so as to estimate the true depreciated yield.

If we assume an industrial building has a 40-year life-span and that when the building is new, the land content is 20% of the value and the initial yield is 7.5%. Thus, using a calculation for each £100 invested, the total investment is £100, less land value at £20 equals a building value of £80. If we depreciate the £80 over a 40-year life, this works out at £2 per annum or 2% of the £100 initial investment. Thus, the true depreciated yield is the 7.5% quoted minus the 2% depreciation which gives 5.5% as a depreciated yield.

The Internet and Changing Business Patterns

The rapid growth of the Internet and its use in business and commerce will have an effect on property markets and the information used in property decisions including valuations. The most important benefits of Internet access are increased competitive advantage, reduced direct communication and information-sharing costs. The surveyor's role as 'information broker' is not seen as being under immediate threat but in the medium to long term, research[14] has suggested that there will be an impact and surveyors will become 'interpreters' and 'managers' of information. There has been scepticism as to whether the web will be used directly for property deals.

Other research has looked at the impact of changing business patterns on the property market. The suggestion is that globalisation, innovation, information and communication technologies, reorganisation of working practices and the drive for flexibility have implications for the demand for business space and the functions of property markets.[15] Changing business patterns, for instance, require more flexible occupational arrangements and lease terms. The leisure market has become more diverse and this has valuation implications. The more uncertain economic environment puts pressure on traditional valuation models and practices.

References

1 Investment Property Databank, *Annual Review 1993*.
2 'Development', *Property Week*, May 5 1994.
3 Baum, A. (ed.) *The Property Industry*, Freeman Publishing, 2000.
4 'Deals: the market picks up', *Property Week*, April 21 1994.
5 King Sturge, *UK Industrial Floorspace Today*, King Sturge, March 2001.
6 *Property Week*, April 21 1994, p. 10.
7 See *supra*, note 3.
8 Lizieri, C. and Richards, P. 'Property Research: Investment', *Estates Gazette*, January 11 1992, p. 77.
9 *Property in a Portfolio Context*, SPR/RICS Technical Seminars Spring 1991.
10 Connellan, O. *Cost Approach to Valuation*, paper presented at RICS valuation techniques seminar, March 13 1992.
11 Colborne, A. *Profits Method*, paper presented at RICS valuation techniques seminar, March 13 1992.
12 Crosby, N. *Reversionary Freeholds: UK Market Valuation Practice*, RICS, 1992.

13 Bowie, N. 'Depreciation: Who Hoodwinked Whom?' *Estates Gazette*, May 1 1982.
14 Royal Institution of Chartered Surveyors, *Building the web: the Internet and the property profession*, Research findings No. 27, RICS, November 1998.
15 Royal Institution of Chartered Surveyors, *Right space, right price? A study of the impact of changing business patterns on the property market*, Research findings No. 14, RICS, October 1997.

Further Reading

A.P. Financial Registers, *Pension Funds and their Advisers*, 1983.
Debenham Tewson & Chinnocks, *Money Into Property*.
Healey and Baker, *Prime Commercial Property Yields*.
Investor Chronicle/Hillier Parker, *Rent Index*.
Jones Lang Wootton, *Index linked gilts and property investment* (Occasional Paper, Summer 1982).
Jones Lang Wootton, *Property Index*.
Jones Lang Wootton, *Office development in Greater London outside the central area* (Technical Paper).
Jones Lang Wootton, *The Decentralisation of Offices from Central London* (Technical Paper).
King & Co., *Industrial Floorspace Survey* (various quarterly).
Plender, J. *That's the way the money goes*, Andre-Deutsch.
Plender, J. 'The £360 bn. Property conundrum', *Financial Times*, December 5 1983.
Property Market Report: Inland Revenue Valuation Office.
Richard Ellis, *Property Market Indicators*.
Various Estates Gazette articles and news stories.

General References and Further Reading

American Institute of Real Estate Appraisers, *Readings in the Income Approach to Real Property Valuations*, Ballinger Publishing Co. 1977.

Bailey, A. *How to be a Property Developer*, Mercury, 1988.

Baum, A. and Crosby, N. *Property Investment Appraisal*, Routledge, 1995.

Baum, A., Mackmin, D. and Nunnington, N. *The Income Approach to Property Valuation*, Thompson Business Press, 1997.

Fraser, W.D. *Principles of Property Investment and Pricing*, Macmillan, 1993.

Isaac, D. *Property Finance*, Macmillan, 1994.

Isaac, D. *Property Investment*, Macmillan, 1998.

Isaac, D. and Steley, T. *Property Valuation Techniques*, Macmillan, 2000.

Johnson, T., Davies, K. and Shapiro, E. *Modern Methods of Valuation* (Ninth Edition), Estates Gazette, 2000.

Jones Lang Wootton/Estates Gazette/South Bank Polytechnic, *The Glossary of Property Terms*, Estates Gazette, 1989.

McIntosh, A.P.J. and Sykes, S.G. *A Guide to Institutional Property Investment*, Macmillan, 1984.

Millington, A.F. *An Introduction to Property Valuation*, Estates Gazette, 1994.

Pinson, B. *Pinson on Revenue Law*, Sweet & Maxwell.

Rees, W.H. *Valuation: Principles into Practice* (Fifth Edition), Estates Gazette, 1980.

Silke, A.S. and Sinclair, W.I. *Hambros Tax Guide*, Hambros.

Stapleton, T. *Estate Management Practice* (Third Edition), Estates Gazette, 1994.

Trott, A.J. *Property Valuation Methods Interim Report*, Polytechnic of the South Bank/RICS.

Turner, D.M. *An Approach to Land Values*, Geographical Publications, 1977.

215

Index